THE RANCH AT LIVE OAK COOKBOOK

DELICIOUS DISHES FROM
CALIFORNIA'S LEGENDARY WELLNESS SPA

THE RANCH AT LIVE OAK COOKBOOK

SUE AND ALEX GLASSCOCK

WRITTEN WITH JEANNE KELLEY AND YSANNE SPEVACK
PHOTOGRAPHY BY SARA REMINGTON
FOREWORD BY CHRISTOPHER KRUBERT, M.D.

RIZZOLI
NEW YORK

New York · Paris · London · Milan

CONTENTS

FOREWORD

My journey with The Ranch began on a nonstop flight from Atlanta to Chicago a few years back. I remember feeling that something was just not right—my back hurt, I felt sluggish, and I just didn't feel like my usual self. As a physician, I had spent years becoming an expert on promoting good health and treating illnesses, but inexplicably, I just didn't feel that healthy. Part of me figured this decline was inevitable for a busy, middle-aged guy. And then, whether by divine intervention or blind luck, I grabbed a copy of *Health* magazine that the last weary traveler had discarded and saw a one-paragraph review of the Ranch at Live Oak. Before I knew it, I was hiking in the Santa Monica Mountains, taking in panoramic views of Malibu and the Pacific, and enjoying a new, intriguing approach to a healthy diet.

There is an ancient Chinese proverb: "He who takes medicine and neglects his diet wastes the skills of his doctors." This simple, yet powerful, testament to the importance of what we put inside our bodies was always something I understood and even advocated to my patients. But as Marc Alabanza, program director of The Ranch, wisely taught me, "Knowing *about* is not the same as *knowing*." You see, reading about the science behind the optimal composition of carbohydrates versus proteins, or reviewing studies on how omega-3s affect the body, is just not the same as experiencing the intelligent, artistic food served at The Ranch.

In the past, young physicians were not trained extensively in how to prevent disease and promote well-being through an optimal diet and nutrition. Of course, we knew that certain food classes were better than others, but it didn't go much further than that. But times are changing. There is an abundance of new research and interest in the medical community regarding how diet, along with exercise, adequate sleep, and other lifestyle choices, can have a major impact on how we feel and perform, and even how long we live.

Food should be part of our joie de vivre, but too many of us have misinterpreted this to mean that dietary bliss and unnatural and indulgent diet go hand in hand. The recipes developed by The Ranch beautifully demonstrate that this is not the case. With minimal fancy culinary technique, they combine nutritionally hyper-dense ingredients to create foods that taste and look spectacular—and most important—are wonderful for you, leaving you full of energy and feeling great. Many guests at The Ranch have talked about "the glow" that occurs after switching from their old diets to this new dietary approach. So, whether you are looking for a complete overhaul of what goes onto your plate or some new recipes to indulge your palate and boost your health, I predict that you and your family will savor the inspiring recipes and ideas in this book for many years to come.

To your health,
Christopher Krubert, M.D.

INTRODUCTION

We created The Ranch at Live Oak in Malibu, California, to provide a special place for people to unplug, recalibrate, and educate themselves about well-being. We run a simple yet highly effective nutrition, fitness, and wellness program that produces measurable results. We strive to be healthy, while living a fun and balanced life. It has been our goal to create a space that is aligned with these values in hope that our guests can make meaningful pattern changes in order to live long, healthy, and vibrant lives.

We have been married for over twenty years, and our journey together is intricately woven into the fabric of this property and the program that we've built. The level of care we take and our personal attention to every detail have allowed us to build an environment for our guests and Ranch staff to thrive. We are passionate about healthy living, and are always excited to discover the latest advancements in wellness, nutrition, consciousness, and exercise.

The Ranch staff members are nothing less than extraordinary and include authorities in every area of exercise, wellness, and nutrition, which benefits the experience of our guests. These include our culinary team, nutritionists, sports and fitness experts, nature guides, yoga masters, chiropractors, acupuncturists, and massage therapists, as well as our hospitality team, whose knowledge and care is the foundation of our program. Together, we've established a healthy living experience that is world-class, and award-winning. Simply put, our program works. It allows people to reset their health and recalibrate their life's direction, and it empowers them to make meaningful life changes.

Optimum nutrition is about eating the very best ingredients and abstaining from, or significantly limiting, the worst. It's about allowing the body to detoxify by avoiding any ingredients that put a strain on digestion or negatively impact the immune system, while adding more of the most nutritious and healthy foods, like vegetables.

Fitness is about being active—so active that your heart rate soars and your blood pounds. It's about having fun with being physical, jumping high, running fast, and building muscle.

Wellness is about deep relaxation, soothing your mind, body, and spirit, and chilling out. It's about appreciating natural beauty internally and externally in our lives, nurturing our own ability to give and receive kindness, cultivating gratitude for every blessing, and living in the moment.

With these three pillars in mind, our guests make deep changes to their health and to their lives. We've seen how our results-based program renews people, helping them shed unwanted pounds, add muscle tone, wean off or significantly reduce prescription medication, and become radiantly healthy, peaceful, and naturally beautiful. Every week we see our guests look younger, feel more confident and empowered, and become energetic, rested, and increasingly effective in their lives. We are more inspired by our guests, as it fulfills our own passionate mission to help them achieve the goals and objectives they desire and make the world a healthier and happier place.

Our guests tell us they love coming to The Ranch—many of them come back every year. And they love eating our cuisine. In fact, they love eating our food so much that they have repeatedly asked us to share our recipes. That's one reason we created the *Ranch at Live Oak Cookbook*. It will enable our guests to continue to eat our food at home year-round.

But that's not the only reason. We're equally driven by a desire to share this essential knowledge as far and wide as possible, to empower as many people as we can to live healthier, more empowered lives, whether they're our guests or people who haven't been able to visit The Ranch in person. We want to support many more people than we can accommodate here in Malibu. With this cookbook, our desire is to share our secrets with a global audience, and to reach out to you. Now you and your family can eat healthful, nutrient-dense foods for optimum health every day.

Our program's three essential pillars—nutrition, fitness, and wellness—work in tandem, and each works best when experienced collectively. If you prepare the recipes in this book but don't get off the couch, you will not experience the extreme vitality of someone who is doing the whole program. Conversely, if you eat terrible food and exercise 24/7, you won't reap the benefits of the exercise. It's our balance of ultimate nutrition, rigorous exercise, and deep relaxation that gets meaningful and sustainable results.

These recipes are at the heart of our program. Our nutrient-dense, plant-based diet has the building blocks you need to lose weight while deeply sustaining your body, all while enjoying rich and interesting flavor profiles.

So, welcome to our world, wherever you are. If you can, come and visit us at The Ranch; if you can't, enjoy some of our great nutritional secrets. With this book, they are now in your hands.

Wishing you health and happiness,
Sue and Alex Glasscock

OUR FOOD PHILOSOPHY

At The Ranch, we believe in delicious foods that are actively good for you. Our vegetarian, organic menu is energy-intensive to sustain the rigorous fitness regime we've developed for our guests. But you don't have to spend a week at our spa to experience this fresh and vibrant low-calorie and enzyme-rich food. The low-gluten, sugar-free recipes that follow are all easily prepared at home for satisfying, irresistible meals that reverse fatigue and build strength. This is spa food that will not only help you lose weight, but detoxify your system and fortify your overall health and well-being.

Our plant-based recipes aren't just enticing and flavorful; these are anti-inflammatory, alkaline foods that balance hormones, blood sugar, and blood pressure. Simple to prepare yet effective, this is hydrating food, rich in the emollient oils that are so good for your skin, nervous system, and brain. They are designed to help relax tired muscles, soothe stress, and comfort you. Suitable for all age groups, these nutrient-dense meals are not only easily digested, but deeply nourishing and sustaining. Wonderfully healing and energy-boosting, these recipes will leave you satisfied, without craving more.

At the end of the book, we've included a three-week results-based meal plan, with recipes for breakfast, lunch, and dinner, all of which were carefully selected to aid in detoxification and weight loss. Our meal plan gives you the tools you need to lose weight and then sustain your ideal weight—along with a new vitality. You'll find that you're excited and inspired to eat healthily—and we predict that many of the recipes in our meal plans will become your daily go-to classics.

The kitchen at The Ranch is truly farm-to-table, but our recipes can be reproduced easily with ingredients found at your local farmers' market and in the organic section of your local grocery store. Our cooking is more about the ingredients we do include—like fresh greens, nuts, and whole grains—and less about what's left out. We suggest seasonal substitutions throughout the book, making these recipes extremely versatile and practical to make year-round.

At The Ranch, our goal is prepare "slow food," not "show food." Slow because the ingredients are always organic, seasonal, and grown as nature intended, often in our own garden. Slow because it's down-to-earth food that's easy to reproduce in a home kitchen without any special skills or hard-to-find garnishes. All you will need are nutritious, delicious, organically grown ingredients. Nothing showy. Nothing fancy.

Of course, many of our high-profile and celebrity guests are repeat visitors to The Ranch because of the simple elegance of our menus. Although they've stayed at other high-end spas around the world, they note that our meals stand apart because they're creative, hearty, and

exciting despite being vegan and low-calorie. We add creaminess with nut milks, abundant flavor with fresh herbs, and create umami notes with ingredients like miso, tamari, and mushrooms—and present it all with a playfulness that our guests always appreciate.

In this solutions-oriented cookbook, we share many of our favorite recipes, along with advice about selecting and cooking with healthy ingredients—information we've gleaned from our years of serving guests at the spa—so that you can re-create The Ranch menus, and enjoy the abundant health benefits, at home, every day.

The Ranch program is challenging on all levels. It's a workout for the mind, body, and spirit, pushing our guests out of their comfort zones and into the freedom that can be found beyond their old fitness levels and familiar surroundings. But there's a delicate balance between pushing against internal boundaries and nurturing ourselves. One of the ways the physical stress is cushioned is by integrating comfort into the meals we serve, a practice that you can implement at home, too.

There are principles that we hold close to our hearts, like eating organic produce, and eating it as freshly picked as possible to enjoy as much of the nutrition and flavor as possible.

And there are a few ingredients that we find ourselves reaching for often, whether it's because they're super nutritious and delicious, or because they're versatile substitutes for things that aren't as healthy.

Here is a selection of principles and ingredients that we truly love.

Eating Organic

The importance (and pleasure) of cooking organic produce cannot be overstated. It's integral to the Ranch philosophy, and if you don't already eat organic, we hope you'll begin to integrate organic foods into your diet, too.

Eating organic is about safeguarding our own and our family's health. It's about avoiding chemical additives and GMOs. It's about eating food that's naturally higher in phytonutrients because it's been grown slowly, without chemical fertilizers speeding up the plants' growth and disrupting their natural uptake and synthesis of nutrition. It's about tree-ripened fruits and vegetables that have grown naturally, unadulterated by chemical pesticides. It's also about trying interesting heirloom varieties that have been bred for flavor, not for productivity and shelf life.

Eating organic is about encouraging biodiversity, protecting honeybees and butterflies and everything above them in the food chain, from birds to beasts, and, ultimately, to humans. It's about caring if our rivers and oceans are free from pesticide residues and if farm animals are humanely reared.

Eating organic is about conserving America's natural beauty, and ensuring that American farmers and farm workers are treated fairly. Eating organic is a vote for American small family farms that truly helps ensure they can survive and thrive. When we eat at a restaurant, we leave tips to show our appreciation, but when it comes to ingredients, the only way we can tip organic farmers is by eating responsibly, shopping at farmers' markets and whole foods stores, and paying a realistic and fair price for the foods we enjoy.

Finally, eating organic is about cooking consciously. It's about continuing the organic approach to food when the ingredients are in your own kitchen. It's about respecting these beautiful foods by cooking them with good intentions and personal responsibility—and enjoying them to the fullest.

Eating Super-Fresh Whole Foods

We believe in whole foods. So often, people think we mean the brand, but we really mean eating as much of every fruit and every vegetable as possible, from the skins to the roots and shoots.

Whole grains, not white grains. Whole dairy, not low-fat dairy. Because we believe that as a part of the natural world, humans fit perfectly into the natural pantry that is all around us and are at our healthiest when eating foods that are from the land, with minimal processing. After all, the most nutritious part of most fruits and vegetables is the skin! And we are fans of eating the highest nutrient content possible.

And we believe in eating fresh. As fresh as you can possibly find. In fact, as fresh as the fresh produce that we grow in our garden, specially for our chef to prepare into fresh meals served within moments of picking.

If you're serious about optimum nutrition and have an outdoor space, we cannot recommend highly enough that you grow an edible garden. The difference in flavor, texture, and nutritional profile is nothing less than extraordinary.

Eating Gluten-Free

Gluten is a protein found in many grains. It's relatively harmless, as can be seen by the fact that people have been eating wheat products for thousands of years. But here at The Ranch, we aren't excited about eating "relatively harmless" food—we're excited about eating food that is actively good for you.

Celiac disease affects a small minority of people. It's an extreme intolerance of gluten that can potentially lead to death. It's serious.

Most people are able to digest gluten with no problems, but there is an increasing body of evidence—both scientific and anecdotal—that even non-celiac digestion processes can be complicated if gluten is present. The stomach feels bloated, and the intestines can become mildly inflamed, resulting in fewer nutrients being absorbed.

It's counterproductive to consume super-nutritious ingredients and simultaneously eat something that prevents us from absorbing them.

Outside of the program, a little gluten can be okay, in the same way that a little alcohol can be okay. But for the Ranch program and for everyday eating, we avoid gluten, if possible.

The Power of Raw

We love eating fresh, organic produce that has as much nutrition, live flora and enzymes, fiber, and flavor in it as possible! In a nutshell, that's why we love eating raw.

We appreciate the beauty of cooked foods, too, in terms of comfort, and also in terms of how the cooking process can sometimes increase the amount of bioavailable nutrients in an ingredient; for example, by cooking quinoa, it's softened and is way more digestible as well as being more delicious and versatile. So we cook quinoa and many other staples, and we don't advocate going totally raw. As a rough guide, we probably eat 50 to 80 percent raw.

In general, most fresh produce has the maximum nutrients in it the moment it is picked. If you've tried freshly picked fruits or vegetables, you'll have experienced just how superior the flavor and texture of this produce is over store-bought. It's incomparable. The fresher the produce, the better.

Eating Superfoods

Superfood is a word that is used to describe any ingredient that is very nutritious. Some superfoods are fruits and vegetables that have a very high phytonutrient level, like blackberries or cauliflower. Other superfoods, such as cacao and maca, are really more like herbal medicines. It's not a food group, like vegetables or grains. It's a way to identify extremely healthy ingredients.

Cooking with All-Natural Sweeteners

At The Ranch, we believe in reducing cravings for sweetness. Nature loves sweetness, but not to the extent that we have become trained to crave it. There's nothing in nature that's as sweet as a can of soda. The only way to obtain an ingredient that sweet is to process something natural and refine it, stripping away any natural nutrients and creating a product that strains the whole body by stimulating a spike in insulin.

For the program, we eliminate refined sugar entirely from the diet in every possible form, and seriously restrict sweetness in the diet, including fruit, fruit juices, dried fruit, agave syrup, honey, maple syrup, and any other sweeteners that contain fructose or glucose.

The only acceptable sweeteners for our program are natural herbs like stevia and mesquite that work differently from anything that's fructose- or glucose-based. The only exception to this is our granola, which helps our guests start their day.

However, if you're not on the program, sweeteners such as honey and maple syrup can be used. These are created with only minimal processing and are therefore whole foods. They are often gentler on the body's insulin production system, and always contain more minerals and nutrients than refined sugar. Though they are high on the Glycemic Index, both are beneficial in small amounts due to their other nutritional components.

Barley malt syrup and brown rice syrup are much lower in glucose and contain complex carbohydrates alongside maltose, so they release into the blood much more slowly and produce much less of an insulin spike. If we loved any sweetener, we'd probably love these the most.

Or stevia, which is a little green herb that looks like mint. It can be found simply dried and powdered, but is most often sold in a more processed form, combined with another sweetener called erythritol.

THINGS WE LOVE

Organic Vegetables

ASPARAGUS: Asparagus spears contain more antioxidants than broccoli—but only if they're freshly harvested (you might want to try growing your own). Even one day after they've been picked, asparagus contains just a quarter of the original nutrients. It's sometimes tempting to use white asparagus spears for aesthetic reasons, but blanched asparagus lacks many of the phytonutrients that make regular green asparagus so good for you. In fact, all blanched vegetables are less nutritious than their unblanched siblings. The more sun a plant is exposed to in the field, the more phytonutrients it has to generate to protect itself from the sun's UV rays, which increases the beneficial nutrients available to us when we eat them.

BROCCOLI: To enjoy the antioxidants and other phytonutrients that naturally occur in broccoli, it's essential to eat very fresh broccoli. Cauliflowers retain their nutrients for a week after being harvested if they're stored in a refrigerator, but broccoli must be eaten within two to three days of being harvested. This means that most broccoli available in the supermarket is past its best. It's not bad for you, but it no longer has its amazing antioxidant content, even if it looks green and fresh. Instead, we recommend that you buy fresh broccoli at the farmers' market, order it through your local Community-Supported Agriculture (CSA) organization, or consider growing your own to ensure that you enjoy all the goodness that fresh broccoli has to offer.

CARROTS: The humble carrot is a vegetable that we use every day. Our guests eat them raw as a little in-between-meals snack. And they're wonderful finely grated into a salad, or used to dip in hummus. They are particularly prized for their cardiovascular health benefits and for their use in protecting the body from cancers, including colon cancer.

Although our grandmothers routinely peeled them, many people now simply scrub them, as the skins contain a lot of beta-carotene. (You'll see that in many of our recipes, we call for unpeeled carrots.) If you want to try eating the whole vegetable, you'll eat the carrot root, its skin, and the greens that grow on top. If you buy carrots from the farmers' market, or grow them yourself as we do at The Ranch, try eating the whole vegetable instead of throwing half of it into the compost!

Purple carrots, now sold in farmers' markets from Union Square to Santa Monica, are a superfood, even more nutritious than the orange variety. Orange carrots were developed by breeding the natural purple pigment out of the vegetable, leaving the orange beta-carotene color. Purple carrots have just as much beta-carotene in them, but also contain a purple pigment, anthocyanin, which is a powerful antioxidant. Anthocyanin is the same stuff that makes blueberries purple, black currants black, and pomegranates red.

CAULIFLOWER: We love cauliflower, including the white cauliflower heads and the greens that grow around the heads and that can be eaten, if you're lucky enough to find a cauliflower that hasn't been trimmed of greens. Surprisingly, white cauliflower heads contain more cancer-fighting phytonutrients than most leafy greens, including lettuce and cabbage. They are also rich in sulfur, which is the beauty mineral. Eat them cooked or raw for glowing skin, strong nails, and lustrous hair.

EGGPLANTS: These contain a type of anthocyanin compound called nasunin, which is believed to protect brain cells; nasunin may have the potential to rebuild brain cells and slow down the brain's aging process.

Eggplants also contain antioxidant phenolics with the potential to protect against free radicals, and therefore protect against degenerative diseases like cancer and coronary diseases. To gain the benefits of these powerful phytonutrients, it's essential to eat the whole vegetable.

FENNEL: Fennel bulbs are rich in heart-healthy phosphorous and in folic acid. They are related to carrots, dill, and parsley, and can be eaten to improve general digestion of other ingredients in a meal. They are naturally pale inside without extra blanching, because the stalks are so tightly packed that the sun cannot penetrate past the outer layers. Fennel has a soothing, carminative effect on the digestion.

GARLIC: This superfood is probably the most potent medicine in your pantry. It boasts a complex array of nutrients and has been used as a medicine for centuries. The two main medicinal compounds in garlic are allicin and quercetin. Allicin is a strong antimicrobial; three cloves of garlic contain the same level of antimicrobial activity as a dose of penicillin. Quercetin has antiviral, antibacterial, and anticancer qualities—and garlic has the strongest cancer-preventing properties of any vegetable, including kale.

Garlic increases physical strength and endurance, making it a perfect ingredient to support the Ranch fitness program. It contains a wonderful natural cocktail of phytonutrients, but in order to get the maximum benefit from them, it's essential to crush the cloves at least 10 minutes before you cook them. The two main medicinal elements inside the juice need time to mix in order for garlic's healing qualities to be ingested at their most potent. As the crushed garlic sits, the flavor also becomes rounder and less harsh. It simultaneously becomes more delicious as the juices get more nutritious—a win-win situation!

GINGER AND TURMERIC: They are closely related, which is why they look so similar and can be used almost interchangeably in recipes. Most fresh ginger sold in markets is old and tough, but strongly flavored. The younger the ginger, the more mildly flavored and tender it is. The youngest ginger has pink tips and is called "stem ginger." It is only found seasonally in spring, and only in specialty health food stores.

Fresh turmeric has just started to appear in whole foods stores; you can find it from February to October. Both ginger and turmeric help the immune system, aid digestion, and are widely praised for their anti-inflammatory properties.

JICAMA: A wonderfully crisp Mexican root vegetable that can be found in Latin American groceries these days, jicama is also available organic at whole foods stores and farmers' markets throughout the country. It tastes delicately sweet, and the texture suggests that it would be high in carbs, but it's not. This white tuber is delicious eaten raw. In fact, it's one of the few vegetables more often eaten raw than cooked. It's destined to become a salad! Like Jerusalem artichokes, it is rich in inulin, which is a prebiotic that helps create the perfect internal environment for your live flora cultures to thrive, and it is also rich in vitamin C, which is great for youthful skin.

KALE: This amazing vegetable strengthens the blood, alkalinizes the whole body, and is a substantial food that provides the main building blocks necessary for the body to make protein. It's become a favorite leafy green for vegans and vegetarians, and a trusted protein builder for omnivores, too. The most nutritious member of the cabbage family, kale is rich in

phytonutrients, including a group called glucosinolates, which give kale powerful protective qualities against cancer (and also nourish skin and nails). Kale is full of antioxidants and minerals—in fact, ounce for ounce, it has more calcium than milk.

With its dark green leaves, Tuscan kale is the most fashionable variety, perhaps because it is the most tender variety, but the leaves of other types of kale can become as soft and flexible when handled correctly. Siberian kale is higher in calcium than Tuscan kale and has a curly leaf around a robust central rib, but the most nutritious varieties are the red ones, including Red Russian kale. All varieties of kale contain the green goodness of Tuscan and Siberian kales, but additionally, the red varieties contain the anthocyanin pigments also found in blueberries, blackberries, pomegranates, and purple carrots.

MUSHROOMS: Not all mushrooms are created equal in terms of their health-promoting properties, but all mushrooms are good for you. Some of the most extraordinary mushrooms can only be found in dried form—dried mushrooms are more potent than fresh ones—and often only powdered. These include reishi and cordyceps, which have incredible phytonutrient profiles. Half a teaspoon of reishi mushroom powder eaten every day is enough to reduce seasonal allergies and raise general immunity noticeably, with increasing effectiveness if eaten regularly for long periods of time. We recommend Jing Herbs Ye Sheng Powdered Reishi Mushroom as a daily supplement; it can be found online or in good health stores.

ONIONS: It's a rare savory recipe that doesn't include an onion for pungent flavor. In addition, onions have medicinal benefits, including increased immunity against colds. But have you ever cooked with a whole, unpeeled onion?

As with garlic, the two main medicinal compounds in onions are allicin, a strong antimicrobial, and quercetin. Quercetin is found in onions in high levels, and has antiviral, antibacterial, and anticancer qualities. Red onions have higher levels of quercetin than yellow onions, and hot onions have much higher levels than sweet onions.

But the onion's skin contains the most allicin and quercetin—as with most vegetables and fruits, the skin is the most nutritious part! Red onion skin is especially fun to cook with, as it can dye the dish a rich burgundy color. Onion skins are too crunchy and tough to consume, of course, but treat them like a bay leaf or a cinnamon stick—add them to a dish as it cooks and remove them before you serve, and you'll reap both the nutritional and culinary benefits.

SEA VEGETABLES: Because we are so beautifully suited to living on this natural planet, and because this planet is mostly covered with ocean, it's no surprise that sea vegetables are so good for the human body. They're grown in the sea, so they're naturally high in minerals as well as the green and red pigments that make field-grown vegetables so good for us.

If you're new to sea vegetables, try dulse first, in perhaps its easiest and mildest form, dulse flakes. Try sprinkling a teaspoon of dulse flakes onto a salad or cooked grains for a little added salty flavor. When you're ready to progress, try arame. It's a beautiful vegetable, its long black strands succulent and delicate with a relatively mild flavor. Nori, best known as the green papery wrap found around sushi rolls, is a wonderful vegetable. It can be used in many ways and is fabulous because it has a great texture as well as a mild taste.

With all sea vegetables, the main concern is buying a brand that's been sourced in oceans that are clean and unpolluted, particularly in waters free from any possible radiation leaks. We recommend eating sea vegetables sourced off the coast of Maine.

SPINACH AND OTHER LEAFY GREENS: Greens such as spinach, romaine, arugula, and dandelion leaves are some of the healthiest vegetables, especially when eaten raw. For greens, choose varieties with the darkest leaf color; these have more lutein, a phytonutrient with antiaging properties that helps the eyes, nerve endings, and the brain. For lettuces, the darker the red, the more anthocyanins they contain, plus dark red lettuces can have more lutein. For all salad greens, fresh is best. Freshly picked spinach leaves have double the phytonutrients than leaves that have been refrigerated for a week. Also, when spinach is boiled, about three quarters of the phytonutrients are lost to the cooking water, so eat the leaves raw, or stir-fry or steam them.

SQUASH: The part of the squash that we call "squash"—the flesh that we typically eat—is a container for the seeds, which are the most precious, not to mention nutritious, part of this vegetable. The second most nutritious part of the squash is the dark stringy material that surrounds the seeds. It's a much darker color than the squash flesh because it has a much higher beta carotene content. Ironically, this is the stuff that usually hits the compost first. The third most nutritious part of the squash is the skin. As with almost all vegetables and fruits, the skin has to protect itself from the sun's damaging ultraviolet rays. Squash skins are thick in texture, and contain more phytonutrients because they have the most contact with the sun's rays. When the skins are eaten, all of these beneficial compounds can be enjoyed for greater health as well as deeper flavor. The least nutritious part of a squash is its flesh, the only stuff that usually makes it onto our plates. It's still nutritious and has amazing flavor, especially when roasted, but when you cook a squash, keep in mind that the flesh is the fourth most nutritious part of this vegetable—and consider incorporating at least the skin into your recipes, too.

Organic Fruits and Berries

BERRIES: They're all full of blue and red anthocyanin compounds, which give them their beautiful colors. Juicy and delicious, berries are high in vitamin C, and they contain the phytonutrients you need to help you to absorb it. They are rich in antioxidants, containing up to two hundred compounds with antioxidant qualities. But that's just the most obvious benefit. Berries universally make us feel and look good, but when it comes to blueberries and blackberries, they truly are superfoods.

Eating fresh or frozen blueberries reverses the physical and mental signs of aging. Our veins become less at risk of blood clots, our heart tissue becomes stronger and more flexible, our blood pressure reduces. Autoimmune diseases and inflammatory diseases are less likely to affect us, and the risk of contracting cancer can be reduced, simply by eating a daily 6-ounce portion of blueberries or blackberries. If you can find them, blackberry cultivars, including boysenberries, marionberries, and loganberries, are as high in phytonutrients, if not higher. Black raspberries are also incredibly good for you and taste amazing.

If you have the space, these berries are all simple to grow, giving you the added benefit of ensuring they are organically grown. Anything related to the blackberry grows like a weed in every climate zone, but blueberries are pickier, preferring an acid soil and cooler climates, and raspberries need coolness, too.

CRANBERRIES: In terms of superfood ranking, fresh cranberries are North America's very own açaí berry. Known to women for the antibacterial qualities that make them effective against urinary tract infections, they can even cure food poisoning because their antibacterial action is so strong. Sweetened cranberry juice and dried sweetened cranberries do contain some of the phytonutrients, but only about a fifth of the power of fresh or frozen cranberries. They're sweetened because the fresh berries are tart, but used creatively, as in the Jicama Salad (page 169) this tartness can be a wonderful addition.

ORANGES: This readily available citrus fruit contains 170 different antioxidant compounds, many of which are found in the skin and pith but not in the juice. The juice is sweeter, and boasts many nutritional benefits, too, because of its rich vitamin C levels, so good for healthy skin and collagen production, but we've included the zest along with the juice in as many of our recipes as possible, because we love whole foods and the flavor and healthy benefits they deliver. The skin and zest don't deserve to languish on the compost pile when they can enhance your well-being (and entice your palate) instead!

Herbs and Spices

Spices aren't just delicious flavorings: they're potent herbal medicines. The spices used in chai were all selected in ancient times by Ayurvedic doctors, the traditional naturopathic medics of India. Here at The Ranch, we're grateful for this ancient heritage, and choose spices known for their ability to assist with the physical processes associated with the program; specifically with fitness, weight loss, and a sense of well-being.

Cinnamon supports the body's response to sugars—it's a must for anyone with diabetes or who is sensitive to sugar as it boosts insulin production. It also lowers cholesterol and triglycerides. Cardamom is a wonderful detoxing spice, and has a strong medicinal quality to support blood health, including helping to prevent blood clots and lowering blood pressure.

Black pepper helps blood circulation, which is so crucial for fitness, and ginger is the primary medicine used in Ayurveda for joint pains. It's an anti-inflammatory, helping relieve conditions such as arthritic rheumatism, jet lag, and allergies, as well as preparing our guests' joints for a strenuous morning hike.

All four of these chai spices also improve digestion, and bring a sense of warmth and comfort, as well as simply being fragrant, exotic, and exquisitely delicious.

We recommend taking herbs called an adaptogens every day. Many herbs are known as adaptogens, and like their name, they help your body adapt to anything. If it's the change of season, they're there to help you adapt. If your life is in transition, they soften the transformation process. As we age, adaptogens support our body's cells in maintaining their vitality. Adaptogens such as ginseng, reishi, astragalus, maca, ashwaganda, or suma are essential resources, and they are incredibly easy to incorporate into our daily lives. Simply add a little adaptogen powder to the almond milk that's poured over your granola every morning, or add it to your smoothie. It's that simple.

Nuts, Beans, and Seeds

CHICKPEAS: Also called garbanzo beans, chickpeas are high in both calcium and fiber. They have a unique texture when cooked, hence their ubiquitous use as a base for hummus, and their mild nutty taste makes them a great addition to entrées needing a light protein.

It may seem counterintuitive to use canned chickpeas rather than making them from the dried beans, but the canning process increases their antioxidant qualities, as well as making

chickpea recipes more convenient to prepare. The high-pressure cooking process used to can chickpeas also makes them softer than home-cooked chickpeas, and makes their nutrients more bio-available.

CASHEWS: These nuts are extremely versatile as a culinary tool. They can be whizzed into cashew milk and cashew ice cream easily, but can never be found truly raw because of the processing that is needed to extract them from the fruit they grow inside, which contains a toxic skin layer around the nut. Cashews contain healthy unsaturated fats, but because The Ranch is a calorie-reduction program, we serve only small portions of cashew-based foods to our guests. Cashews are about 50 percent fat, which makes a 1-ounce portion of the raw nuts 175 calories. Thankfully 1 ounce goes a long way!

PEPITAS: These are simply the seeds found in the center of a pumpkin or winter squash. They are rich in vitamin E, and are particularly good for male health, including protecting against male forms of cancer. Try roasting them in tamari for a quick and nutritious snack, or simply eat them raw. They can also be made into pepita milk using the almond milk recipe in this book. Simply replace the almonds for pepitas on a 1:1 ratio and with the same quantity of water.

SESAME SEEDS: Sesame is a versatile food in every variation, including the raw and toasted seeds, as an oil, and as tahini. It's usually served as the topping on a bun, but that's a shame, as it has incredible healing benefits. Sesame plants are related to devil's claw, a medicinal herb used to treat rheumatoid arthritis, tendinitis, and joint pains in the knees, hips, and lower back. Sesame seeds aren't as strong in their action, but they do contain enough anti-inflammatory qualities to help protect guests as they intensively work out on The Ranch's demanding exercise program. They're also high in copper compounds, which again are great for relieving arthritis pains. Tahini is simply pulverized sesame seeds. It's basically a nut butter, but made with seeds. Nothing added, nothing taken away, it contains the whole goodness of sesame seeds but is easier to digest.

Grains

BROWN RICE: We only recommend brown rice, as white rice is the same grain, but with the most tasty, nutritious, and beneficial parts removed! Every length and size of brown rice is nutritious, including brown basmati and short-grain brown rice, and all are naturally gluten-free.

Brown rice is high in manganese, an essential mineral that helps digest fats, and is also helpful for digesting proteins and carbohydrates. As it's full of complex carbohydrates, it is a great fuel for sustained energy. Wild rice is a completely different and unrelated food, and it's not truly rice at all, but a pseudo-grain. It's native to Minnesota, and is a healthy natural food that is seasonal and delicious.

MILLET: Gluten-free and delicious, millet is a super alkaline food, and is rich in the magnesium your body needs for healthy muscle production and nerve cell function. It has an anti-inflammatory effect that's perfect for our guests as they prepare for exercise, or recover from a long day.

There are many varieties of millet, including popping millet that's fun to heat and serve just like popcorn, with sea salt, spices, or herbs. Regular millet can be cooked into a grain with individual seeds, like quinoa, or can be cooked with more water to make a sticky paste. It can also be made into a porridge by grinding the grains first. Alternatively, soak and sprout it to enjoy all the raw health benefits and sprouting greens.

QUINOA AND KANIWA: These two related Andean pseudo-grains are both, in fact, seeds. That's why they're so nutritionally rich compared with true grains, like wheat and barley, and are naturally gluten-free. They are almost identical in nutritional profile, the main differences being that kaniwa is smaller and is not covered in the bitter powdery film that coats quinoa.

The most nutritious part of any grain is the germ, with the rest of the seed made up of carbohydrates and fiber. In wheat, the germ is about 3 percent of the seed; in quinoa and kaniwa, it's about 60 percent. This is another reason why it's so much more nutritious.

Quinoa and kaniwa contain all of the essential amino acids, so they are a complete protein food as well as containing complex carbohydrates. They contain a compound that is thought to help stabilize blood sugar and reduce the risk of diabetes, and also helps trigger brain chemicals that make you feel full and satiated.

There are many varieties of quinoa available, including red and black. As with most foods, the black variety is the most nutritious, as it contains anthocyanins, the same pigment in blueberries that make them such a great antioxidant food.

OATS: These are the original gluten-free weight-loss superfood. All oats are naturally gluten-free, so why are some labeled as "Gluten-Free Oats"? Some oats are grown in fields used for wheat in the previous season. A few stragglers may grow from dormant wheat seeds that hadn't germinated the previous year, and when the current year's oats are harvested, a small percentage of the harvest could possibly be contaminated with this wheat. Gluten-free oats are guaranteed to have been grown in wheat-free fields. Also, they're guaranteed to be rolled, steel-cut, and packaged in a facility that doesn't process gluten-containing grains. But unless you have celiac disease, the quantities of gluten contamination from oats that aren't certified as gluten-free is so tiny that you should feel free to eat them.

Oats are great for weight loss, because they're high in both soluble and insoluble fiber. Both types of dietary fiber bring a sense of fullness and satisfaction without the calories. Soluble fiber also lowers your blood cholesterol and glucose levels, sustaining you for longer after breakfast. Insoluble fiber keeps your digestive tract healthy, not just through maintaining regularity, but also because it helps create a perfect internal environment for your unique live cultures to flourish. Healthy internal flora leads to deep health in every aspect of your body, including dental health, strengthened immunity, and a healthy heart.

Fermented Foods

Although many people in the United States do not regularly eat fermented foods, they are an essential part of a healthy diet, as many Asian cultures have long known. Most pickled vegetables are now made simply by steeping them in an acid—for example, vinegar—but traditional pickles were made by steeping the vegetables in salt water for long enough that the vegetable's own lactic acid created a pickling medium acidic enough to process the vegetable. Pickling vegetables the traditional way allows us to absorb more of the phytonutrients because the vegetables' cell walls are perforated during the lacto-fermenting process. Additionally, the live cultures fermented foods contain keep us healthy long after the pickles have been digested. Eating fresh, living cultures is an essential practice for good health; it's probably the second most crucial part of a vegetarian diet, topped only by eating fresh leafy green vegetables. Cultivating a balance of live cultures internally ensures that there's less room inside our bodies for pathogens and other "bad bacteria." And it means we have plenty of the "good guys" inside our bodies to do all sorts of helpful symbiotic tasks, including things like manufacturing vitamin B_{12}, which is essential for nerve health and for keeping our minds sharp as we age.

But take note: Pickles are best for you if they're made by bruising the vegetables and leaving them to ferment in brine, as opposed to the more common method of leaving them to steep in vinegar. Traditionally, all fermented vegetables were made in this way, from kimchi to sauerkraut to the classic New York pickled cucumber. Fermented veggies are simple to make, as you'll see from the Pickled Red Onions recipe (page 109). However, if you buy fermented vegetables, check the ingredients. Pickling foods in vinegar doesn't nurture the live cultures

found in truly fermented foods. The preference is an ingredient list that only includes the vegetable, brine, herbs, and spices.

TAMARI: Soy sauce can be found very easily, but the difference between regular soy sauce and artisan tamari and shoyu is as profound as the difference between sliced white bread and a home-baked whole-grain loaf, or a bottle of artisan wine and a box of bad wine. The flavors and the health benefits are huge, because they are made from such different processes.

Regular soy sauce is an industrial product made without fermentation. Tamari and shoyu are artisan products made in the time-honored way through fermentation, and have different grades, just like wine.

The main difference between tamari and shoyu is that tamari is made from fermented soy beans, and shoyu is made from fermented soy beans and wheat berries. This is why tamari is always gluten-free, and shoyu is not. For the program, we only recommend tamari, as we are a gluten-free center, but for general year-round eating, we consider shoyu to be a healthy food unless you eat a strict gluten-free diet or have celiac disease. Tamari is strong in antioxidant compounds and in vitamin B$_3$, which is great for easing joint pain and arthritis. That's one of the reasons it's a wonderful ingredient for our physically active guests. It also contains an amino acid called tryptophan, a gentle mood enhancer, which can help with the midweek challenges of being away from family and home.

As with all fermented foods, tamari supports internal colon health by helping replenish the biotic cultures in the intestines essential for so many of the body's processes. While some people prefer to avoid tamari due to its high sodium content, we find this another useful reason for our guests to enjoy this whole food, as it helps avoid muscle cramps during this intensive exercise program.

APPLE CIDER VINEGAR: One of the most versatile foods, apple cider vinegar is the basis for many of the oil-free dressings served at most meals at The Ranch. We only use unpasteurized and unfiltered apple cider vinegar, because the pasteurization and filtering processes remove the most beneficial part of the vinegar, which is the live culture.

Fermented foods are all about eating live cultures to replenish the live culture strains that live inside the belly. Research suggests that eating apple cider vinegar has huge health benefits from this action, including helping to control weight.

As a detoxing ingredient, it's second only to pure water. Apple cider vinegar is never drunk undiluted, but a teaspoon in a glass of water adds to the detoxing properties of the water, flushing the body of toxins and unwanted heavy elements of a poor diet.

It's rich in potassium, the main element that supports electrolyte levels in the body and therefore muscle and cardiac function. This is another reason it's wonderful for our guests—it supports them as they exercise.

From a culinary perspective, we use apple cider vinegar to add intense flavor to our plant-based recipes, giving them the level of flavor that our guests often only associate with non-vegetarian dishes. This way the vinegar is also able to support weight loss, purely by making low-calorie and low-fat recipes more delicious and, therefore, more satisfying.

Raw Agave Nectar

Agave nectar has a wonderful prebiotic action, creating a perfect internal environment for beneficial active cultures to thrive. Make sure you choose raw agave nectar, which is much harder to find than the regular agave syrup that has been a source of much controversy in recent years. Raw agave nectar is clear and has a gelatinous consistency, like aloe vera gel. Reject any agave nectar that looks like maple syrup, as this is not authentic raw agave, which is a naturally produced, healthful ingredient.

The brand we recommend is Sweet Ojio Raw Organic Agave Syrup, which is widely available online, in selected health food stores, and at Whole Foods markets. However, even raw agave syrup is high in fructose and should be eaten in moderation.

start the day

THE RANCH GRANOLA

Every spa has a signature granola recipe, but guests find our granola especially irresistible due to its unique cookie-like texture—it's all about the crunch!—and malty maple syrup flavor. We love switching out the nuts and dried fruit, for example, swapping in raw cashews for the walnuts, or golden raisins for the dried apricots.

Makes about 20 cups (40 servings)

INGREDIENTS

Unrefined virgin coconut oil, for brushing

6 cups walnut halves

4 cups steel-cut oats

2 cups pecan halves

2 cups almonds, chopped

1¼ cups sunflower seeds

2 cups unsweetened shredded coconut

1 tablespoon ground cinnamon

2 teaspoons freshly grated nutmeg

8 large egg whites

1¾ cups maple syrup

1 cup dried blueberries

1 cup dried apricots, chopped

1 cup dried dates, chopped

Preheat the oven to 250°F. Brush a rimmed baking sheet with coconut oil.

In a large bowl, using your hands, mix the walnuts, oats, pecans, almonds, sunflower seeds, coconut, cinnamon, and nutmeg.

In a medium bowl, gently whisk the egg whites and maple syrup with a fork, taking care to keep the foam to a minimum. Pour the egg white mixture over the dry ingredients and mix with your hands to evenly coat.

Transfer the granola mixture to the baking sheet, spreading it out so that the layer is slightly thicker toward the sides. This will prevent the granola at the edges from sticking during baking. Bake the granola mixture for about 25 minutes, then rotate the baking sheet and bake for 25 minutes more. Remove from the oven, carefully mix the granola with a spatula, and then bake for another 25 to 30 minutes, until golden brown.

Let cool, then add the dried blueberries, apricots, and dates and mix thoroughly to combine. (The granola can be stored in an airtight container for up to 2 weeks.) Serve as a wholesome breakfast with homemade almond milk (see page 44).

EACH ½-CUP SERVING *364 calories (kcal) • 23 g fat • 0 mg cholesterol 32 g carbohydrates • 6 g dietary fiber • 10 g protein • 38 mg sodium • 47 IU vitamin A trace vitamin C • 57 mg calcium • 2 mg iron*

VARIATION *Try dipping large chunks of this granola into our raw Chocolate Mousse (page 205), and then freeze them. Once the chocolate has set around the granola, it becomes a delicious, actively healthy chocolate energy snack.*

SPICED CRANBERRY-HAZELNUT GRANOLA

Sprinkle this light, flaky, cereal-style granola over sliced fresh fruit or applesauce or enjoy a small bowl of it moistened with almond milk or fruit juice. The cinnamon, nutmeg, and orange zest will wake up your taste buds.

Makes about 10 cups (about 40 servings)

INGREDIENTS

4 cups rolled oats

2 cups chopped hazelnuts

1 cup coconut chips

½ cup ground flaxseed

1 teaspoon ground cinnamon

½ teaspoon freshly grated nutmeg

¾ teaspoon sea salt

¾ cup unrefined virgin coconut oil, plus more for brushing

¾ cup pure maple syrup

Zest and juice of 1 medium-size orange

1 tablespoon pure vanilla extract

1 cup dried cranberries

Preheat the oven to 350°F. Brush two heavy rimmed baking sheets with coconut oil.

In a large bowl, mix the oats, hazelnuts, and coconut chips with the flaxseed, cinnamon, nutmeg, and salt.

In a medium saucepan, combine the oil, syrup, orange zest and juice, and vanilla extract. Bring to a simmer over medium heat. Pour the syrup over the dry ingredients in the bowl and stir with a heatproof spatula to evenly coat.

Divide the granola mixture between the baking sheets and spread to form a single layer. Bake for 15 minutes, remove from the oven, and stir. The granola near the edges of the pan will begin to brown more quickly than the middle, so move the granola on the edges to the middle of the pan and vice versa.

Continue to bake, stirring every 10 minutes, until the oats and nuts are golden brown, about 20 minutes longer. Add the cranberries, mix thoroughly to combine, and let cool before serving. (The granola can be stored in an airtight container for up to 1 week.)

EACH ¼-CUP SERVING *159 calories (kcal) • 10 g fat • 0 mg cholesterol 15 g carbohydrates • 2 g dietary fiber • 3 g protein • 46 mg sodium 3 IU vitamin A • 0 mg vitamin C • 19 mg calcium • 1 mg iron*

THE RANCH ALMOND MILK

Forget about cartons of almond milk. If you make only one recipe from this book, this one has the greatest power to transform your life. For starters, fresh almond milk tastes a thousand times better than the kind that comes from cartons, and it's no wonder: Flip the carton on its side and check out the ingredients list—it's long and often includes something called "potassium citrate" or "vitamin A palmitate" that you'd never find in your kitchen, as well as added flavors even in the unflavored kind. Our almond milk takes just 2 minutes to make and the ingredients are simple. Almonds. Water. A little sweetener. Plus some adaptogen powder if you're so inclined.

But here's the truly transformative part: Almond milk is more hydrating for your body than pure water. Not only does it contain water, which is of course your best friend, but it also provides essential fatty acids that keep your cells hydrated and flexible. For optimum hydration, we recommend drinking 1 to 2 quarts of this milk per day.

For straining the almond milk, an essential step, you can use either a muslin bag or a nut-milk bag, specifically made for straining nut milks.

Makes about 1 quart

INGREDIENTS

1 cup raw almonds, soaked, if possible (see Tip)

1 tablespoon raw agave nectar, or to taste

Adaptogen powder, such as ginseng, reishi, astragalus, maca, ashwaganda, or suma (optional; see Note)

If you have time, soak the almonds in water to cover for 4 to 8 hours; discard the soaking water.

Place the soaked or raw almonds and 3 to 4 cups water in a blender, along with the agave nectar and adaptogen powder, if using. Blend at the highest setting for about 2 minutes (the milk will still have some solid pieces of almond).

Place a strainer or colander over a large bowl and line it with muslin. Pour the blended almond mixture through the muslin so that any solid ground almonds remain in the cloth, but the liquid almond milk drains into the bowl. When all of the liquid has drained through the cloth, gather up the edges, lift it out of the strainer or the colander, and squeeze it thoroughly to extract all of the almond milk into the bowl.

Drink immediately or bottle the milk and refrigerate for 4 or 5 days. Shake the bottle if it separates. If you choose to add maca powder to your almond milk, drink it within a few hours to ensure freshness. Maca has a strong flavor, so consider adding a little more agave, too.

EACH 1-CUP SERVING 89 calories (kcal) • 7 g fat • 0 mg cholesterol
4 g carbohydrates • 2 g dietary fiber • 3 g protein • 3 mg sodium
1 IU vitamin A • 0 mg vitamin C • 52 mg calcium • 1 mg iron

COOK'S TIP *We recommend keeping a container of nuts soaking in the refrigerator so you always have soaked nuts on hand. This recipe will work if the nuts aren't soaked, but it's healthier, creamier, and more delicious if the almonds are soaked first.*

INGREDIENT NOTE *These nutrient-dense herb powders are optional, but we highly recommend that you add them to your almond milk every day (the amount will vary depending on the herb; check dosage recommendation for each). The good fats that are suspended in the almond milk help your body absorb the benefits of these superfoods much more efficiently.*

VARIATIONS *For increased creaminess, we recommend adding ½ teaspoon vegan, non-soy lecithin, which is available at natural food stores or online. Derived from plant membranes, this yellowish fatty substance supports cardiovascular health, flexibility, and memory. Avoid soy lecithin, a by-product of highly processed soy foods made from GMO sources.*

To make a delicious vanilla almond milk, simply add ½ teaspoon natural vanilla extract; blend to combine.

FRESH TURMERIC-AND-SPICE-INFUSED ALMOND MILK

Fresh turmeric has an exotic, earthy, floral-citrus flavor that pairs beautifully with other spices in this flavored almond milk—look for the small, orange, gingerlike roots at natural foods stores or at Indian or Thai markets. The spice infusion can be made ahead and kept in the refrigerator so that you can mix a single serving whenever you desire. Think of this beverage as a caffeine-free chai and serve it hot or chilled.

Turmeric has long been used in Indian Ayurvedic medicine to treat skin conditions, and contemporary research confirms its impressive anti-inflammatory properties, as well as its antifungal and antibacterial powers. Initial studies are also finding that curcumin, a substance found in turmeric, may be effective in slowing the growth of cancer cells, treating rheumatoid arthritis, and even warding off the onset of Alzheimer's.

Makes 8 servings

INGREDIENTS

1 (2-inch) piece cinnamon stick

6 cardamom pods

3½ ounces unpeeled fresh turmeric root

8 cups almond milk, homemade (page 44) or unsweetened store-bought

About 8 teaspoons raw agave nectar

In a small, heavy saucepan, combine 1 cup water, the cinnamon, and the cardamom. Bring to a rolling boil over high heat, then reduce the heat to maintain a simmer and cook for 20 minutes. Place the turmeric root in a blender, add the hot spice mixture, and pulse briefly until the turmeric and spices are finely chopped. Let stand until cooled.

Strain the turmeric-spice infusion through a fine-mesh sieve into a jar, pressing firmly on the solids to extract as much liquid as possible; discard the solids. (The turmeric-spice infusion can be made up to 2 weeks ahead. Seal the jar tightly and refrigerate.)

For each serving, in a glass combine 1 cup almond milk, 1 tablespoon turmeric-spice infusion, and 1 teaspoon agave nectar and stir to blend.

EACH SERVING *80 calories (kcal) • 3 g fat • 0 mg cholesterol 13 g carbohydrates • 1 g dietary fiber • 1 g protein • 150 mg sodium 500 IU vitamin A • 0 mg vitamin C • 201 mg calcium • trace iron*

RAW OATMEAL
WITH ALMONDS AND FRUIT

Every commercial for heart-healthy breakfast cereal advertises the soluble fiber found in oats. But while store-bought breakfast cereals generally also contain processed ingredients, including ample amounts of sugar, that may be harmful to your health, this super-simple raw oatmeal recipe contains only the purest ingredients: heart-healthy oats (which also contain insoluble fiber, great for increasing healthy intestinal flora), cinnamon, and almonds sweetened with dried fruits that are all softened during an overnight soak. No need to add dairy creamer or even almond milk—the oat flour diffuses into the water, creating a creamy oat milk. This is old-fashioned Swiss-style know-how, but with a modern twist that infuses even more nutrition and a little more style into your cereal. Simply prepare this oatmeal before you go to bed at night and it'll be ready to eat come breakfast time.

Makes 1 serving

INGREDIENTS

2 dried plums (we love French Agen plums; see Note)

5 raw almonds

1 cup rolled oats

½ teaspoon ground cinnamon, plus more for sprinkling

¼ to ½ small apple

Pit and chop the dried plums. With a sharp paring knife, roughly chop the almonds.

Put the oats into a single-serving bowl, top with the plums and nuts, and sprinkle with the cinnamon. Pour 2 cups lukewarm water over the dry ingredients to immerse them. Cover the bowl with a plate and set aside on the counter overnight.

The next morning, remove the plate and, using a box grater, grate the fresh apple on top. Sprinkle with additional cinnamon, if desired, and serve immediately.

EACH SERVING *385 calories (kcal) • 8 g fat • 0 mg cholesterol*
72 g carbohydrates • 11 g dietary fiber • 11 g protein • 1 mg sodium
152 IU vitamin A • 1 mg vitamin C • 33 mg calcium • 4 mg iron

INGREDIENT NOTE *Dried plums and prunes are the same thing, but they are typically labeled as dried plums when they're made from a special cultivar of plum, such as Agen, Kakadu, Ageleno, or damson. Whatever the variety, dried plums are very high in antioxidants due to the anthocyanins that give them their dark color. They also contain sorbitol, a strong probiotic compound that promotes the growth of desirable flora inside your body. Eating plenty of natural plant fiber, found in foods like oats and dried plums, may reduce your need to take commercial probiotic capsules—these natural foods will keep your internal cultures in balance. However, if you've been taking antibiotics or are feeling run down, probiotic capsules are a good idea.*

VARIATIONS *Try adding a little ground vanilla bean or ¼ teaspoon pure vanilla extract to the oats before soaking them. This recipe is also delicious prepared with walnuts or raw pecans instead of almonds.*

OATS AND TEFF WITH CARDAMOM AND PEACHES

Teff, a poppy seed–size grain from Ethiopia, is rich in protein, calcium, and iron. You can find this gluten-free cereal at natural foods stores and at supermarkets with good gluten-free sections. Combined with heart-healthy oats and spice, teff makes for a comforting porridge that's a great start to the day. If peaches are not in season, try topping this hot cereal with pears, strawberries, or bananas.

Makes 4 servings

INGREDIENTS

½ to 1 teaspoon kosher salt, as desired

½ cup steel-cut oats

½ cup teff

1 teaspoon ground cardamom

2 small peaches, pitted and sliced

Almond milk, homemade (page 44) or unsweetened store-bought, for serving

Bring 4 cups water and the salt to a boil in a heavy medium saucepan over high heat. Stir in the oats, teff, and cardamom. Reduce the heat to low and simmer, stirring occasionally, until the porridge is thick and creamy, about 30 minutes. Divide the porridge among four bowls. Top with the peaches and serve with almond milk.

EACH SERVING *182 calories (kcal) • 2 g fat • 0 mg cholesterol 37 g carbohydrates • 6 g dietary fiber • 6 g protein • 245 mg sodium 212 IU vitamin A • 4 mg vitamin C • 46 mg calcium • 3 mg iron*

TIBETAN TSAMPA

Tibet is a beautiful mountainous country, with a traditional cuisine that suits its remote, high-altitude terrain. Nutritionally dense, the diet found in this Himalayan region is deliciously earthy and grounding, and so it lends itself well to cooler days at The Ranch, when the Santa Monica mountains become misty as the marine layer rolls in from the Pacific Ocean. It's incredibly beautiful and makes this hearty dish all the more welcoming, whether it's served at breakfast time or as a comforting dessert after a long day's hike, just as the Tibetan sherpas enjoy it!

Roasting the barley and milling it as described in this recipe results in a tsampa that's well worth the effort. The flour keeps well in an airtight container in the fridge, so consider making a big batch. However, if you need a shortcut, here's how to quickly toast store-bought barley flour: Heat a cast-iron skillet over high heat, add a cup of barley flour, and toast it, stirring continuously with a wooden spoon, for about 1 minute. As soon as you can detect a slight brown color and the smell of toasted malt, transfer the toasted flour to a large cold bowl—it will cool on contact. Repeat with more flour; you'll need 1¾ cups to make this tsampa.

Makes 6 servings

INGREDIENTS

1 (1-inch) piece fresh ginger, grated (optional)

4 teaspoons unrefined virgin coconut oil, melted

½ cup dried goji berries (see Note)

2 cups hull-less barley grains, washed (see Note)

8 cups almond milk, homemade (page 44) or unsweetened store-bought

1 cup unsweetened coconut yogurt or almond milk, for serving (optional)

½ cup dried apricots, chopped

6 tablespoons barley malt syrup

If using the grated ginger, stir it into the coconut oil and set aside in a small bowl to infuse. In another small bowl, combine the goji berries with enough water to cover and set aside to reconstitute.

Place the barley in a strainer in the sink, heat a pot of water to boiling, and pour it over the grains. Cover the strainer with a clean cloth and set aside for about 20 minutes, until partially steamed. Remove the cloth and spread it out on a flat surface. Spread the barley on the cloth in a thin layer and let it stand for about 10 minutes to cool and dry.

Heat a large cast-iron skillet or a wok over high heat, add the barley, and toast it, stirring continuously with a wooden spoon, for about 5 minutes. Some of the grains will open at the seams with a pop. Transfer the grains to a cold bowl when they smell roasted, but before they burn; the bowl will cool the barley on contact, ending the toasting process.

Grind the barley in a coffee grinder, flour mill, or a high-speed blender until it becomes a flour.

In a large pot over a medium-high heat, bring the almond milk and infused coconut oil to a boil. Add the roasted barley flour, ½ cup at a time, stirring with a wooden spoon or whisk until all the flour has been incorporated. Lower the heat and continue to cook for about 5 minutes, until the mixture thickens into a creamy porridge.

Serve in individual bowls, topped with the coconut yogurt, if using, the drained reconstituted goji berries, chopped apricots, and barley malt syrup.

EACH SERVING, WITHOUT COCONUT YOGURT *363 calories (kcal) • 7 g fat 0 mg cholesterol • 68 g carbohydrates • 8 g dietary fiber • 8 g protein • 261 mg sodium • 935 IU vitamin A • 1 mg vitamin C • 301 mg calcium • 2 mg iron*

INGREDIENT NOTES *Goji berries are one of the traditional Tibetan superfoods we recommend to our guests for their revolutionary antiaging, antioxidant, and cholesterol-lowering qualities—and they're high in vitamin A and beta-carotene, too. They have a lovely flavor, more subtly sweet than most dried berries without the tartness or acidity, and a short soak in water gives them a delicate texture.*

Barley is surprisingly high in protein, and its ability to support the body to lower cholesterol and protect heart health is well documented. This is especially true when the whole grain is eaten, as with hull-less barley, which retains both its bran and germ layers. Steaming whole hull-less barley removes the enzyme inhibitors, transforming complex starches into barley malt. It's the malt that gives this traditional barley cereal its delicate sweetness.

VARIATIONS *You can substitute honey for the malt syrup, if preferred, or dairy milk for the almond milk. Dried goji berries and apricots are a wonderful match for barley's malt flavor, but feel free to switch out the dried fruit for any other variety you like.*

SWEET AND CHEWY MULTIGRAIN FRUIT AND NUT BARS

Gluten-free and vegan, these slightly sweet, nutty, fruity bars are the perfect grab-and-go breakfast or snack. With loads of fill-you-up fiber and high-satiety nuts, one bar will keep you going all day. Take them to work, or on a hike or any sort of adventure. Brown rice syrup, available at natural foods stores, is derived from cooked brown rice and has a low glycemic index, plus it's super sticky and perfect for holding all the goodness of the bars together. You'll want to use hulled sunflower seeds for the recipe—sometimes these are labeled "seeds" and sometimes "kernels," which is what they technically are.

Makes 16 bars

INGREDIENTS

2 cups rolled oats

½ cup raw almonds, coarsely chopped

½ cup raw pecans

¼ cup millet

¼ cup unrefined virgin coconut oil, plus more for brushing

1½ cups puffed brown rice

¾ cup unsweetened shredded coconut

½ cup coarsely chopped dried sour cherries

½ cup golden raisins

¼ cup roasted unsalted hulled sunflower seeds

2 tablespoons toasted flaxseed

1 cup brown rice syrup

2 tablespoons light molasses

1 teaspoon kosher salt

Preheat the oven to 400°F.

On a large, heavy, rimmed baking sheet, combine the oats, almonds, pecans, and millet. Toast the oat mixture in the oven until the oats are just golden, about 6 minutes. Set aside the oat mixture to cool, and reduce the oven temperature to 325°F.

Meanwhile, brush a 9-inch square baking pan with coconut oil, and then line the pan with parchment paper so that the paper extends up over two edges of the pan. Brush the parchment with coconut oil.

Generously brush a large bowl with coconut oil. Add the cooled oat mixture, puffed rice, shredded coconut, cherries, raisins, sunflower seeds, and flaxseeds and stir to combine.

In a heavy, deep saucepan, combine the coconut oil, brown rice syrup, molasses, and salt. Bring the syrup mixture to a boil and continue boiling for about 1 minute. Immediately pour the boiling syrup over the oat mixture in the bowl. Using a silicone spatula, stir until the oat mixture is evenly coated with the syrup.

Transfer the oat mixture to the prepared pan. Using the same spatula, press the mixture to form an even layer in the pan, and then smooth the top. Bake the bars for 10 minutes. Turn the pan and continue baking until the bars are golden brown in the center with slightly darker edges, about 15 minutes longer.

Cool in the pan completely, and then cut into 16 bars. To remove the bars from the pan, grab hold of the parchment extending over the sides of the pan. The bars can be prepared up to 4 days ahead; wrap them individually in waxed paper and store in resealable plastic bags.

EACH BAR *301 calories (kcal) • 12 g fat • 0 mg cholesterol*
44 g carbohydrates • 5 g dietary fiber • 5 g protein • 160 mg sodium
144 IU vitamin A • 0 mg vitamin C • 39 mg calcium • 2 mg iron

GLUTEN- AND SUGAR-FREE BANANA BREAD

Medjool dates add sweetness to this moist g-free quick bread, replacing the granulated sugar in most banana bread recipes. For snack time, enjoy the banana bread unadorned—it's delicious on its own and chock-full of luscious banana flavor. Coconut oil adds nutty sweetness and is a healthy alternative to the butter found in most banana bread.

For breakfast, cut the loaf into thick slices, spread with peanut butter, and top with rounds of ripe banana (see variation, below).

Makes 1 loaf (12 servings)

INGREDIENTS

⅓ cup unrefined virgin coconut oil, melted and cooled slightly, plus more for brushing

3 very ripe large bananas

6 large moist Medjool dates, pitted

1 large egg

1⅓ cups gluten-free flour

1 teaspoon baking soda

½ teaspoon kosher salt

1 tablespoon unfiltered apple cider vinegar

Position an oven rack in the center of the oven and preheat the oven to 350°F. Lightly brush an 8½ by 4½ by 4¾-inch loaf pan with coconut oil.

In the bowl of a food processor with the metal blade attachment, puree the bananas and dates until smooth. Add the egg and coconut oil and pulse until combined. Mix in the flour, baking soda, and salt, and then mix in 3 tablespoons water and the vinegar; the batter will be thick yet pourable. Transfer the batter to the prepared pan.

Bake until the bread is golden brown and a toothpick or tester inserted into the center comes out clean, about 55 minutes. Cool the bread in the pan on a wire rack for 10 minutes, then turn the loaf out onto the rack and cool completely. (The bread can be prepared up to 3 days ahead. Wrap tightly in plastic wrap and keep in a cool place.)

EACH SERVING, BREAD ONLY *165 calories (kcal) • 7 g fat • 14 mg cholesterol 27 g carbohydrates • 2 g dietary fiber • 2 g protein • 201 mg sodium 59 IU vitamin A • 3 mg vitamin C • 11 mg calcium • trace iron*

VARIATION *To make open-faced peanut butter and banana sandwiches, slice the bread into ½-inch-thick slices. Spread each slice with about 1½ tablespoons peanut butter. Arrange banana slices on top of the peanut butter, about 5 pieces of banana on each slice of bread, and serve.*

AVOCADO TOASTS WITH MICRO GREENS AND SESAME

Rich in potassium, folic acid, and vitamin K, creamy avocados are a satisfying toast topper that makes a quick breakfast or lunch. The recipe calls for Asian micro greens, which are a blend of sprouted herbs, mustard, and radish, but it is tasty with any micro mix. The robust toasted sesame oil expands the Asian flavor profile.

Makes 2 servings

INGREDIENTS

2 slices multigrain or
gluten-free bread, toasted

1 ripe avocado, pitted, peeled, and sliced

¼ lemon, cut into 2 wedges

Kosher salt and freshly ground
black pepper

½ cup Asian micro-mix salad or
other micro greens

½ teaspoon toasted sesame oil

2 teaspoons sesame seeds, toasted

Arrange the toast on plates and top with the avocado slices, dividing them equally. Using a butter knife, gently mash the avocado slices onto the toast. Squeeze the lemon wedges over the avocado and sprinkle with salt and pepper. Divide the micro greens evenly over the avocado. Drizzle ¼ teaspoon sesame oil over each toast, sprinkle each with 1 teaspoon sesame seeds, and serve.

EACH SERVING *253 calories (kcal) • 16 g fat • 0 mg cholesterol 22 g carbohydrates • 7 g dietary fiber • 4 g protein • 148 mg sodium 867 IU vitamin A • 31 mg vitamin C • 46 mg calcium • 5 mg iron*

SWEET POTATO MUFFINS WITH COCONUT CRYSTALS

Sweet potato muffins, spiced and fresh from the oven, are a happy fall and winter indulgence. This gluten-free version has a delectable caramelized topping of coconut crystals—a type of raw sugar made from coconut. Look for the crystals at natural foods stores where they are sometimes also labeled as coconut sugar.

Makes 12 muffins

INGREDIENTS

1 cup sweet potato puree, made from baked or steamed peeled sweet potatoes

2 large eggs

½ cup pure maple syrup

½ cup unsweetened applesauce

⅓ cup unrefined virgin coconut oil, melted and cooled slightly

1 teaspoon pure vanilla extract

2 cups gluten-free flour

¼ cup ground flaxseed

2 teaspoons baking powder

1 teaspoon baking soda

1 teaspoon ground cinnamon

½ teaspoon sea salt

½ teaspoon ground allspice

¼ cup coconut crystals, for garnish

Preheat the oven to 400°F. Line a 12-cup muffin tin with unbleached paper muffin liners.

In a medium bowl, whisk together the sweet potato puree, eggs, maple syrup, applesauce, coconut oil, and vanilla to blend.

In a large bowl, whisk together the flour, ground flaxseed, baking powder and soda, cinnamon, salt, and allspice to blend. Add the wet ingredients to the dry ingredients and use a spatula to fold together; do not overmix.

Divide the batter among the prepared muffin cups. Sprinkle with the coconut crystals. Bake until the tops are brown and a toothpick inserted into the centers comes out clean, about 22 minutes; do not overbake. Cool completely before serving.

EACH MUFFIN *214 calories (kcal) • 8 g fat • 31 mg cholesterol 34 g carbohydrates • 1 g dietary fiber • 3 g protein • 306 mg sodium 1,896 IU vitamin A • 1 mg vitamin C • 71 mg calcium • 1 mg iron*

BLUEBERRY-ALMOND OAT MUFFINS

Here's a lightly sweet and moist version of the breakfast favorite that everyone can love—the gluten sensitive and bakery buffs alike. Almond flour, found at natural foods stores and some supermarkets, adds a pleasant nuttiness and texture.

Makes 12 muffins

INGREDIENTS

1 cup gluten-free flour

1 cup almond flour

¼ cup rolled oats, plus
3 tablespoons for garnish

¼ cup ground flaxseed

2 teaspoons baking powder

1 teaspoon baking soda

1 teaspoon ground cinnamon

½ teaspoon kosher salt

1 cup almond milk, homemade (page 44) or unsweetened store-bought, or coconut milk from a carton

½ cup pure maple syrup

⅓ cup unrefined virgin coconut oil, melted and cooled slightly

2 large eggs

1 teaspoon pure almond extract

1 cup fresh blueberries

Preheat the oven to 400°F. Line a 12-cup muffin tin with unbleached paper muffin liners.

In a large bowl, whisk together the gluten-free and almond flours, oats, flaxseed, baking powder and soda, cinnamon, and kosher salt to blend.

In a medium bowl, whisk the almond milk, maple syrup, coconut oil, eggs, and almond extract to blend. Stir in the blueberries. Add the wet ingredients to the dry ingredients and use a spatula to gently fold together; do not overmix. Let the batter stand until it thickens slightly, about 5 minutes.

Divide the batter among the prepared muffin cups. Sprinkle the tops with the remaining 3 tablespoons oats. Bake until a toothpick inserted into the centers comes out clean, about 20 minutes; do not overbake. Cool completely before serving.

EACH MUFFIN *212 calories (kcal) • 12 g fat • 27 mg cholesterol 24 g carbohydrates • 2 g dietary fiber • 4 g protein • 311 mg sodium 88 IU vitamin A • 1 mg vitamin C • 99 mg calcium • 1 mg iron*

BUCKWHEAT-FLAX PANCAKES
WITH WALNUTS AND MAPLE SYRUP

These gluten-free pancakes are a Sunday favorite at The Ranch—especially after an early morning hike. Walnut oil lends rich, nutty flavor, light texture, and omega-3 fatty acids to the flapjacks. A short stack is also delicious with a sliced banana in place of the strawberries.

Makes about 24 (4-inch) pancakes

INGREDIENTS

⅔ cup rolled oats

2 tablespoons roasted flaxseeds

¾ cup buckwheat flour

1¼ cups almond milk, homemade (page 44) or unsweetened store-bought

1 large egg

1 large egg white

2 teaspoons baking powder

Scant 1 teaspoon sea salt

2 tablespoons pure maple syrup, plus more for serving

1 tablespoon walnut oil, plus more for brushing

¼ cup finely chopped walnuts

1 pint strawberries, hulled and sliced

Combine the oats and flaxseeds in a blender and pulse until ground into a coarsely textured flour. Add the buckwheat flour, almond milk, egg, egg white, baking powder, and salt and blend until the batter is well mixed. Blend in the maple syrup and walnut oil.

Brush a griddle or well-seasoned cast-iron skillet with walnut oil and heat over medium-high heat. Spoon about 2 tablespoons of the batter onto the griddle, creating a 4-inch pancake. Repeat with more batter, evenly spacing the pancakes so they don't crowd the griddle. Sprinkle the top of the pancakes with the chopped walnuts, about ½ teaspoon per pancake. Cook the pancakes until a few holes appear on the surface and the bottoms are browned, about 3 minutes. Using a spatula, carefully flip the pancakes over and cook until the second sides are golden brown, about 1 minute. Transfer the pancakes to serving plates and repeat with the remaining batter. Serve with maple syrup and the strawberries.

EACH SERVING (2 PANCAKES) *96 calories (kcal) • 4 g fat • 16 mg cholesterol 11 g carbohydrates • 2 g dietary fiber • 4 g protein • 267 mg sodium 75 IU vitamin A • 0 mg vitamin C • 75 mg calcium • 1 mg iron*

BLISTERED TOMATO AND SPINACH SCRAMBLE

We sear the tomatoes in a hot skillet to concentrate their flavor before stirring them up with other offerings from the garden. You can make this scramble with eggs or a combination of whole eggs and whites if you want to reduce calories and saturated fat. Nutritional yeast, available at natural foods stores, adds a Parmesan cheese–like finish to this satisfying breakfast or brunch dish.

Makes 4 to 6 servings

INGREDIENTS

4 teaspoons extra-virgin olive oil

1 pint grape tomatoes (about 2 cups)

1 garlic clove, minced

6 cups lightly packed spinach leaves

½ cup chopped scallions

1 tablespoon chopped fresh thyme

Pinch of crushed red pepper flakes

Salt and freshly ground black pepper

6 large eggs (or 3 large eggs plus 4 egg whites), beaten to blend

Nutritional yeast, for sprinkling (optional)

Heat 2 teaspoons of the oil in a large, heavy, well-seasoned skillet over medium-high heat. Add the tomatoes and the garlic and cook, shifting the pan occasionally, until the tomatoes are lightly browned and blistered on all sides, about 4 minutes. Transfer the tomatoes to a bowl.

Add the remaining 2 teaspoons oil to the same skillet (do not wash) and return to medium-high heat. Add the spinach, scallions, thyme, and red pepper flakes to the skillet and sauté until the spinach is tender, about 5 minutes. Distribute the spinach evenly over the surface of the skillet. Scatter the blistered tomatoes over the spinach and sprinkle with salt and black pepper to taste. Pour the eggs over the vegetables in the skillet and turn off the heat. Immediately stir the egg mixture with a heat-proof spatula until the eggs are gently scrambled, about 1 minute. Serve the scramble hot and sprinkle with nutritional yeast, if desired.

EACH SERVING (BASED ON 6 SERVINGS) *103 calories (kcal) • 6 g fat 93 mg cholesterol • 6 g carbohydrates • 2 g dietary fiber • 7 g protein • 114 mg sodium 1,361 IU vitamin A • 19 mg vitamin C • 43 mg calcium • 2 mg iron*

BERRY BREAKFAST SMOOTHIE

This smoothie is all about the berries—whether you choose strawberries, blueberries, raspberries, or blackberries (or some delightful combination), they're all full of blue and red anthocyanin compounds, natural pigments that give them their beautiful colors. Juicy and delicious, berries are also high in vitamin C, and they contain the necessary phytonutrients to help you to absorb it. Though they are all rich in antioxidants, which help to slow down the aging process, and protect the body against cancer and other inflammatory diseases, blueberries and blackberries top the charts, boasting up to two hundred compounds with antioxidant qualities—so enjoy these superfoods whenever you have the opportunity.

Makes 2 (10-ounce) servings

INGREDIENTS

1 cup fresh or frozen berries (strawberries, blueberries, raspberries, blackberries, or a combination; see Note)

½ cup freshly chopped kale leaves (remove the stalks before chopping)

¼ cup chopped broccoli

½ banana

½ cup diced fresh pineapple

½ avocado, pitted and peeled

About 1 cup fresh orange juice

In a blender, place the berries, kale, broccoli, banana, pineapple, and avocado. Slowly add the orange juice to the blender carafe, ¼ cup at a time, pulsing to blend. Continue adding more juice and pulsing to blend until you've reached the smoothie consistency you like. Serve immediately, as the nutrients in this smoothie diminish over time.

EACH SERVING *165 calories (kcal) • 8 g fat • 0 mg cholesterol 25 g carbohydrates • 7 g dietary fiber • 3 g protein • 14 mg sodium 2,065 IU vitamin A • 105 mg vitamin C • 55 mg calcium • 1 mg iron*

INGREDIENT NOTE *Eating fresh or frozen blueberries or blackberries helps reverse the physical and mental signs of aging. Our veins become less at risk of blood clots, our heart tissue becomes stronger and more flexible, our blood pressure goes down. We are less likely to develop autoimmune or inflammatory diseases simply by eating a daily 6-ounce portion of these marvelous berries.*

GINGERED PINEAPPLE, CELERY, AND ROMAINE SMOOTHIE

Leaf green and very refreshing. We appreciate this nutrient-packed drink at The Ranch for the anti-inflammatory qualities found in pineapple. If you haven't chopped a fresh pineapple before, here's how: Using a large, serrated knife, cut the leafy top and the bottom from the pineapple. Place the pineapple with the bottom cut side down on the cutting board and trim away the rind following the contour of the fruit with the knife. Cut the pineapple lengthwise into quarters and slice away the core. Refrigerate prepared pineapple in an airtight container until ready to use.

Makes 1 serving

INGREDIENTS

1 cup pineapple chunks (from about ¼ small pineapple)
1 cup lightly packed romaine lettuce leaves
½ cup sliced celery (about 1 stalk)
1 (1¼-inch) piece fresh ginger, peeled

In a blender, puree the pineapple, romaine, celery, and ginger with ¼ cup water until smooth. Serve immediately.

EACH SERVING *126 calories (kcal) • 0 g fat • 0 mg cholesterol
32 g carbohydrates • 4 g dietary fiber • 2 g protein • 46 mg sodium
4,411 IU vitamin A • 21 mg vitamin C • 65 mg calcium • 1 mg iron*

JUICE VARIATIONS

Juicing is an easy way to get your daily requirements of fruits and vegetables.

Some juicing machines remove the juice and leave behind the pulp, which has fiber and helps fill you up. So add the pulp back into the juice or use it in cooking.

When juicing, make only as much juice as you can drink in one day. Fresh-squeezed juice can quickly develop harmful bacteria. Make sure to wash the blender or juice machine thoroughly.

The health benefits of juicing are similar to eating whole fruits and vegetables. Pure, raw juice contains essential vitamins, minerals, and phytonutrients found in the whole fruit. Current research is looking into juicing's effectiveness in reducing the risk of cancer, boosting the immune system, aiding digestion, and helping to lose weight.

SHINE ON! JUICE

This vitamin A–intense blend of carrots, citrus, and pineapple has a spicy ginger jolt and a cool, crisp finish from fresh romaine lettuce. Chia seeds can be added for increased fiber and protein.

Makes 1 serving

INGREDIENTS

1 (1-inch) piece fresh ginger, peeled
1 orange, peeled, pith and seeds removed
2 carrots, unpeeled
1 stalk celery

1 lime, peeled, pith and seeds removed
1 cup pineapple chunks
(from about ¼ small pineapple)
1 head romaine lettuce
1 tablespoon chia seeds (optional)

Juice the ginger, orange, carrots, celery, lime, pineapple, and lettuce; stir in the chia seeds, if using, and serve.

EACH SERVING *179 calories (kcal) • 4 g fat • 0 mg cholesterol*
36 g carbohydrates • 7 g dietary fiber • 4 g protein • 52 mg sodium
10,606 IU vitamin A • 107 mg vitamin C • 155 mg calcium • 2 mg iron

WAKE-UP! KALE JUICE

When juicing vegetables it is always good to add a fruit. A crisp apple adds some sweetness.

Makes 1 serving

INGREDIENTS

1 apple, unpeeled

½ bunch kale, stems removed

1 beet, trimmed and peeled

1 grapefruit, peeled, pith and seeds removed

1 medium cucumber, unpeeled

1 lemon, peeled, pith and seeds removed

Pinch of cayenne pepper

Juice the apple, kale, beet, grapefruit, cucumber, and lemon; stir in the cayenne and serve.

EACH SERVING *147 calories (kcal) • 0 g fat • 0 mg cholesterol 34 g carbohydrates • 5 g dietary fiber • 5 g protein • 70 mg sodium 6,451 IU vitamin A • 111 mg vitamin C • 135 mg calcium • 2 mg iron*

GO GREEN! JUICE

Greens are mellowed by kiwis and cucumber; flaxseed adds texture and protein.

Makes 1 serving

INGREDIENTS

Leaves and tender stems from ½ bunch fresh parsley

2 kiwi fruits, peeled

1 green apple, unpeeled

1 orange, peeled, pith and seeds removed

1 medium cucumber, unpeeled

½ bunch Swiss chard, stems removed

1 bunch spinach, stems removed

1 tablespoon ground flaxseed

Juice the parsley, kiwi, apple, orange, cucumber, chard, and spinach; stir in the flaxseed and serve.

EACH SERVING *202 calories (kcal) • 3 g fat • 0 mg cholesterol 44 g carbohydrates • 8 g dietary fiber • 6 g protein • 168 mg sodium 6,439 IU vitamin A • 163 mg vitamin C • 169 mg calcium • 5 mg iron*

soups and salads

WHOLE LEEK SOUP

The allium family includes hundreds of varieties of onions, shallots, scallions, and garlic. It also includes the leek, a less ubiquitous cousin of the onion that has the benefits of a rounder flavor profile, green goodness in its upper leaves, and a little more cachet for being less well known. Here, we keep the flavors intact by using the whole vegetable and keeping the seasonings minimal.

Makes 2 servings

INGREDIENTS

6 baby leeks or 2 large leeks

2 tablespoons extra-virgin olive oil

1 (1-inch) piece kombu (see Note)

Sea salt and freshly ground black pepper

Rinse and chop off the roots of the leeks and set aside. Slice the leeks lengthwise almost in half, from the top of the leaves to the middle of the white portion, keeping the halves together.

Open each leek under running water to wash out any dirt; alternatively, open them in a big bowl of water to clean them. Be sure to clean the root as well.

When they're thoroughly washed, chop the leeks into ½-inch-thick slices, cutting the upper parts into half rounds and the lower parts into rounds. Finely chop the roots.

In a soup pot, heat the oil over medium heat. Add the leek roots and sauté for about 3 minutes. Add the rest of the leeks, cover the pot, and sauté for about 5 minutes. Stir with a wooden spoon, replace the lid, and sauté for about 5 minutes more. Add 4 cups water and the kombu, raise the heat to high, and bring to a boil. Lower the heat to maintain a simmer, and continue simmering the soup until the leeks are very soft, about 20 minutes.

Remove the kombu and season the soup with salt and pepper. Let the soup sit for about 10 minutes before serving.

EACH SERVING *181 calories (kcal) • 14 g fat • 0 mg cholesterol 13 g carbohydrates • 2 g dietary fiber • 1 g protein • 27 mg sodium 1,484 IU vitamin A • 11 mg vitamin C • 55 mg calcium • 2 mg iron*

INGREDIENT NOTE *Kombu is edible kelp from Japan. The dried, greenish-black seaweed comes in small square pieces, which are excellent for adding flavor to soups and stocks. Find at natural foods stores and Japanese markets.*

VARIATIONS *This soup tastes fresh and fragrant with a handful of finely chopped tarragon leaves added at the end. Alternatively, garnish with finely chopped chives or garlic chives, which are richer in allicin, a more powerful antimicrobial compound, measure for measure, than any other member of the onion family.*

WHOLE ONION AND CARROT SOUP

Probably the most universally agreed upon direction for a healthy diet is to eat whole foods. The main ingredients in this delicious soup all should be used whole: the onion and the garlic clove, whose skins are the most nutritious part of all, and the carrots: use the root with its skin and the greens that grow on top. We especially love purple carrots, which are rich in the beta-carotene found in the orange variety, but also anthocyanin, a strong antioxidant.

Makes 6 servings

INGREDIENTS

4 large red onions, unpeeled

1 whole head garlic

1 bunch parsley

1 bunch carrots (use purple carrots, if available), unpeeled, green tops attached

3 bay leaves

½ teaspoon finely ground pink Himalayan salt

¼ teaspoon freshly ground black pepper

Leaves from 1 bunch cilantro

Remove any stickers and packaging from the onions and cut them in half. Don't remove the skins or roots from the onions, and leave the skin on the head of garlic as well.

In a large stockpot over a high heat, bring 6 cups water, the onions, whole garlic head, and half the parsley (both leaves and stems) to a rolling boil, then lower the heat, cover the pot, and simmer until the onions and garlic are tender and the onion broth is richly flavored, about 30 minutes.

Meanwhile, remove the green tops from the carrots and set aside. Scrub the carrot roots but don't peel them, then roughly chop them into ½-inch chunks.

Using a slotted spoon, carefully remove the onion, garlic, and parsley from the pot, leaving behind the onion broth. Discard the herbs and garlic, but leave the onion halves to cool on a cutting board. Add the chopped carrots and the bay leaves to the pot and return the broth to a boil.

Meanwhile, carefully remove and discard the skins from the cooked onions. The skins will come away very easily, but use a paring knife to pry apart the skin from the roots and the tops of the onions. In a blender, combine the cooked onions with a little of the broth and blend for about 10 seconds to make a rough puree; you want to retain some of the texture of the onions. Add this puree to the soup pot and continue simmering for another 10 minutes.

Roughly chop the tough stems of the carrots into ½-inch-long pieces (kitchen scissors are helpful here), then chop the feathery tops separately and place in a bowl; reserve. Add the stems to the soup and simmer until they are tender, about 10 minutes.

Add the chopped carrot tops to the soup along with the salt and pepper. Simmer the soup until the carrot tops soften, about 10 more minutes. Use a knife to remove the leaves from the remaining parsley. Take the soup off the heat, add the parsley and cilantro leaves, and let the soup sit, covered, to allow the flavors to meld, about 5 minutes.

Serve immediately, or store in the refrigerator overnight. As with most soups, this is even better the next day.

41 calories (kcal) • 0 g fat • 0 mg cholesterol
10 g carbohydrates • 2 g dietary fiber • 1 g protein • 197 mg sodium
8,277 IU vitamin A • 10 mg vitamin C • 32 mg calcium • trace iron

CREAMY VEGAN TOMATO AND BASIL SOUP

Warming and rich, this vegan tomato soup is transformed by cashews, which are blended into the soup for creamy perfection.

Makes 4 to 6 servings

INGREDIENTS

1 cup raw cashews, soaked in water to cover for 1 to 4 hours

¼ cup extra-virgin olive oil

2 medium yellow onions, finely chopped

6 medium garlic cloves, minced

2½ pounds tomatoes

1 quart low-sodium vegetable broth

2 bay leaves

½ cup loosely packed fresh basil leaves, finely chopped

1 teaspoon sea salt

½ teaspoon freshly ground black pepper

Drain the cashews, discarding the soaking liquid. Transfer the nuts to a blender along with 1 cup fresh water. Blend for about 1 minute, until the cashew cream is completely smooth; set aside.

In a large soup pot, heat the oil over low to medium heat. Add the onions and garlic and sauté until the onions are translucent, about 10 minutes. Add the tomatoes, raise the heat slightly, and continue to cook until the onions and tomatoes are completely softened and sweet tasting, 15 to 20 minutes.

Add the broth, bay leaves, basil, salt, and pepper and cook over medium heat until the vegetables are very tender, about 30 minutes more. Remove and discard the bay leaves. Carefully transfer the hot soup to the blender, add the cashew cream (see Variations), and blend until the soup is creamy. Serve immediately.

EACH SERVING (BASED ON 6 SERVINGS) *281 calories (kcal) • 20 g fat 0 mg cholesterol • 21 g carbohydrates • 3 g dietary fiber • 6 g protein • 512 mg sodium 1,468 IU vitamin A • 35 mg vitamin C • 70 mg calcium • 3 mg iron*

VARIATIONS *Reserve a little of the cashew cream and garnish the soup with a swirl of the cream and a sprinkle of additional finely chopped basil. And why not play with the seasonings? This soup is equally delicious made with fresh marjoram or thyme instead of the basil; ½ teaspoon paprika makes a wonderfully smoky addition.*

GOLDEN SESAME SEA VEGETABLE SOUP

Minerals are the newest area of health research, and sea vegetables are full of them, including trace minerals. Kelp is the easiest sea vegetable to start eating, as it has no flavor. Nori is the sweetest sea vegetable and also the most familiar—it's wrapped around sushi rolls. Dulse has a mild flavor and a thin, delicate texture that's almost papery. It's also available as dulse flakes, which are used like grated Parmesan. This creamy, dairy-free, deeply nourishing soup tastes wonderful and looks fabulous, like a little bowl of warm molten gold speckled with dulse rubies.

Makes 4 servings

INGREDIENTS

1 cup sesame seeds, soaked in 2 cups water for 2 to 6 hours

1 (4-inch) piece fresh turmeric, 4 teaspoons fresh turmeric juice, or 4 teaspoons ground turmeric

1 cup kelp noodles, rinsed and drained

Sesame oil

1 medium shallot, peeled and thinly sliced

1 cup nori flakes

1 cup dulse flakes

½ cup finely chopped fresh dill, or 1 tablespoon dried dill, plus more chopped fresh dill for garnish

Sea salt and freshly ground black pepper

Drain the soaked sesame seeds, discarding the soaking water. In a high-speed blender, puree the sesame seeds with 4 cups fresh water. Add the turmeric and blend at high speed until well combined.

With kitchen scissors, cut the kelp noodles into approximately 2-inch pieces and place in a large bowl. Cover with the sesame puree and set aside.

Heat a thin layer of oil in a soup pot over medium heat. Add the sliced shallot and sauté for a few minutes, lowering the heat if necessary so that the shallot turns translucent but doesn't brown. Add the sesame and kelp mixture to the pot and gently bring to a simmer, stirring. Reduce the heat to low, cover the pot, and simmer for about 20 minutes, or until the kelp noodles are soft.

Remove the pot from the heat, add the nori, dulse, and dill, and stir thoroughly. Let the soup stand to allow the flavors to meld, about 5 minutes. Taste and season with salt and pepper, if necessary. Serve in soup bowls, garnished with fresh dill.

EACH SERVING *268 calories (kcal)* • *21 g fat* • *0 mg cholesterol*
12 g carbohydrates • *5 g dietary fiber* • *10 g protein* • *177 mg sodium*
285 IU vitamin A • *4 mg vitamin C* • *246 mg calcium* • *5 mg iron*

CAULIFLOWER SOUP

While following the program at The Ranch, guests dine on this low-carb but highly satisfying soup. It's served rib-sticking thick, similar to a puree, but at home you can add more broth for a soupier bowl. Garnish it with cilantro, scallions, red pepper, or all three.

Makes 4 servings

INGREDIENTS

2 teaspoons extra-virgin olive oil

1 small onion, sliced

2 garlic cloves, chopped

2 teaspoons curry powder

¼ teaspoon turmeric powder

1 large head cauliflower, cut into 1-inch florets

4 cups low-sodium vegetable broth, plus more if needed

Salt and freshly ground black pepper

Chopped fresh cilantro, for garnish (optional)

Sliced scallions, for garnish (optional)

Crushed red pepper flakes, for garnish (optional)

Heat the oil in a large heavy saucepan over medium heat. Add the onion and garlic and sauté until tender and golden, about 10 minutes. Stir in the curry and turmeric powder and cook until fragrant, about 1 minute.

Add the cauliflower and broth. Cover and simmer until the cauliflower is very tender, about 30 minutes. Set 1 scant cup cooked cauliflower florets aside. Carefully transfer the remaining cauliflower mixture to a blender and puree until smooth, adding more broth if necessary to thin. Return the cauliflower puree and reserved florets to the saucepan and season to taste with salt and pepper. (The soup can be prepared 4 days ahead; cover and refrigerate.)

Bring the soup to a simmer over medium heat, stirring occasionally. Once the soup is heated through, ladle into bowls and garnish with cilantro, scallions, and red pepper flakes as desired.

EACH SERVING *100 calories (kcal) • 3 g fat • 0 mg cholesterol*
15 g carbohydrates • 5 g dietary fiber • 4 g protein • 195 mg sodium
trace vitamin A • 88 mg vitamin C • 75 mg calcium • 2 mg iron

TOFU, CABBAGE, AND MISO SOUP

Tofu sometimes gets a bad rap, but this recipe will change your mind. Our tofu soup is delicious because the tofu is marinated in Asian flavorings that are both healthful and sensationally sensuous. Garlic, ginger, red shiso, crushed red pepper flakes, and sesame seeds give this dish antioxidant power while raising the bar on how fabulous a tofu soup can be. The miso kicks it up another notch in terms of nutritional prowess as well as flavor.

Makes 4 servings

INGREDIENTS

1 (13-ounce) block tofu,
cut into ½-inch cubes

2 large garlic cloves, crushed

1 (2-inch) piece fresh ginger, finely grated

4 fresh red shiso leaves (see Note),
finely chopped

½ teaspoon crushed red pepper flakes,
or to taste

2 tablespoons black sesame seeds,
plus more for garnish

5 tablespoons miso paste

2 scallions

1 tablespoon sesame oil

2 cups cabbage greens, such as
shredded cabbage, chopped turnip tops,
or arugula (see Note)

Nori flakes, for garnish

Put the cubes of tofu in a nonreactive bowl. Add the garlic, ginger, shiso, crushed red pepper, and sesame seeds and mix with your hands to coat the tofu thoroughly.

Mix 1 tablespoon of the miso paste with 1 cup hot water until well combined and the mixture forms a thick sauce. Pour the sauce over the tofu mixture and mix until well combined. Set aside to marinate for at least 30 minutes or, for the best flavor, refrigerate overnight.

When you're ready to proceed, remove the tofu from the refrigerator. Trim and discard the roots from the scallions and chop into 1-inch pieces on an angle.

In a soup pot, heat the sesame oil over medium heat, add the scallions, and sauté for 2 minutes. Add the tofu mixture and cook for another 4 to 5 minutes, stirring continuously. Add 4 cups water to the pot and bring to a boil. Stir in the cabbage greens, lower the heat to maintain a simmer, and cover the pot. After 5 minutes, remove the lid and check if the cabbage greens are tender. If not, continue to simmer for a few minutes more until the greens are the desired texture.

Remove the pot from the heat. In a small bowl, combine ¼ cup of the cooking broth with the remaining 4 tablespoons miso paste. Using a spoon, mash the paste against the side of the bowl and mix well with the broth to form a thick sauce. Add more broth to the bowl, ¼ cup at a time, until you have a thin sauce with a gravy-like consistency. Add the sauce to the pot, stir well, and let the soup sit for 5 to 10 minutes to allow the flavors to meld.

Serve the soup hot, garnished with nori flakes and additional black sesame seeds.

EACH SERVING *186 calories (kcal)* • *9 g fat* • *0 mg cholesterol*
17 g carbohydrates • *5 g dietary fiber* • *10 g protein* • *647 mg sodium*
149 IU vitamin A • *20 mg vitamin C* • *149 mg calcium* • *1 mg iron*

INGREDIENT NOTE *Red shiso is a kind of basil. It's a versatile herb that we like to add to raw salads and any dish that calls for basil. Red shiso leaves can be found in Asian markets, but feel free to substitute Thai basil leaves or any type of readily available fresh basil in this recipe.*

INGREDIENT NOTE *There are many varieties of cabbage to try, including pointed spring cabbage, Savoy cabbage in winter, and red cabbage throughout the year. Arugula, radish, and turnip greens are also candidates for this soup, as they're all members of the cabbage family and contain the cruciferous family of phytonutrients that can help protect the body from cancer.*

RADICCHIO AND KOHLRABI SALAD WITH AVOCADO AND EGG

Kohlrabi, a member of the cabbage family, can be cooked or eaten raw in salads or slaws. The flavor is similar to that of a broccoli stem, but milder and slightly sweeter—it's at its best when paired with the slightly bitter radicchio, creamy avocado, and rich egg in this salad.

Makes 4 servings

INGREDIENTS

2 large eggs

2 tablespoons extra-virgin olive oil

1 tablespoon white wine vinegar

1 tablespoon white balsamic vinegar

2 teaspoons Dijon mustard

¼ teaspoon sea salt

1 small head radicchio, torn into bite-size pieces (about 4 cups)

1 large kohlrabi, trimmed, peeled, and cut into matchsticks

1 large avocado, pitted, peeled, and diced

Freshly ground black pepper

2 teaspoons chopped chives for garnish (optional)

Place the eggs in a small pot, cover with water, bring to a gentle simmer, and continue to simmer slowly for 5 minutes. Remove the eggs from the heat, cover, and let stand for 5 minutes. Rinse the boiled eggs under cold water to cool, and then refrigerate until well chilled. (The eggs can be cooked up to 1 week ahead and refrigerated.)

In a small bowl, whisk together the oil, both types of vinegar, the mustard, and the salt to blend. Arrange the radicchio, kohlrabi, and avocado on four plates. Peel the eggs, coarsely chop them, and sprinkle over each salad. Drizzle each salad with dressing, top with the chives, if using, and finish with the pepper.

EACH SERVING *159 calories (kcal) • 11 g fat • 81 mg cholesterol 11 g carbohydrates • 6 g dietary fiber • 6 g protein • 249 mg sodium 217 IU vitamin A • 70 mg vitamin C • 48 mg calcium • 1 mg iron*

MEXICAN FRUIT SALAD WITH CHILI SALT

A refreshing take on the fruit salad—it's a perfect hot afternoon pick-me-up, Mexican dinner side dish, or even a cool and spicy dessert. Mexican papayas are the large variety—the same kind found in Thailand, with yellow-green-orange skins and pinkish-orange flesh when ripe. Papayas contain the enzyme papain, which has been shown to benefit and aid digestion. Look for Mexican papayas at Latin American and Asian markets.

Makes 6 servings

INGREDIENTS

1½ pounds Mexican papaya
(about ½ medium papaya),
peeled, seeded, and sliced

¾ pound jicama (about ½ medium jicama),
peeled and chopped into ½-inch-thick sticks

1¼ pounds watermelon
(about ¼ mini watermelon), sliced

¼ large pineapple, peeled, cored, and sliced

1 large mango, pitted, peeled, and sliced

1 cucumber, peeled and sliced

3 limes, halved

1 teaspoon ground ancho pepper
or other medium-hot ground pepper

½ teaspoon sea salt

2 tablespoons finely chopped
fresh cilantro leaves (optional)

In a shallow serving dish or bowl, arrange the papaya, jicama, watermelon, pineapple, mango, and cucumber. Squeeze the limes over the fruit and sprinkle with the ancho pepper and salt. Sprinkle with the cilantro, if using, and serve.

EACH SERVING *117 calories (kcal) • 0 g fat • 0 mg cholesterol*
29 g carbohydrates • 5 g dietary fiber • 2 g protein • 169 mg sodium
1,674 IU vitamin A • 92 mg vitamin C • 38 mg calcium • 1 mg iron

HEARTS OF PALM AND WATERCRESS WITH BALSAMIC DRESSING

Watercress is peppery, freshly foraged even more so. It is a flavor that is beautifully tamed by mellow hearts of palm, the sweetness of the dried currants, and the crunch of the toasted nuts.

Makes 2 to 4 servings

INGREDIENTS

¼ cup extra-virgin olive oil

2 tablespoons balsamic vinegar

1 teaspoon good-quality red wine vinegar

Pinch of crushed red pepper flakes

1 teaspoon minced garlic

2 tablespoons dried currants

Sea salt and freshly ground black pepper

1 large bunch watercress, ends trimmed (3 to 4 cups)

1 (14-ounce) can hearts of palm, drained and cut into ⅓-inch-thick slices

2 tablespoons pine nuts, toasted (see Tip)

2 thin slices red onion, separated into rings

In a medium bowl, whisk together the oil, both types of vinegar, the crushed red pepper, and the garlic to blend. Mix in the currants. Season the dressing with salt and black pepper.

Add the watercress, hearts of palm, and pine nuts to the dressing and toss to coat. Divide the salad among plates. Top each salad with red onion and serve.

EACH SERVING (BASED ON 4 SERVINGS) *222 calories (kcal) • 17 g fat 0 mg cholesterol • 15 g carbohydrates • 2 g dietary fiber • 5 g protein • 112 mg sodium 1,396 IU vitamin A • 26 mg vitamin C • 49 mg calcium • 1 mg iron*

COOK'S TIP *Due to their small size and high fat content, pine nuts can go from golden to burned in a second. It's safest to toast them on the stove where you can keep your eye on them. Toast pine nuts in a cast-iron skillet over medium heat, stirring continuously, until golden brown, about 2 minutes. Transfer immediately to a small bowl.*

RANCH CAPRESE WITH CASHEW CHÈVRE

Juicy heirloom tomatoes meet creamy vegan goat cheese in this heavenly take on a traditional Italian salad. A blend of rich cashews with a touch of herbs, garlic, and lemon is remarkably similar to fresh chèvre. Plan ahead: The chèvre must be started at least 2 days in advance. Micro basil is tiny, just-sprouted basil with mild flavor. Find micro basil where you look for other fresh herbs at your specialty foods store or search out the micro greens stand at your local farmers' market.

Makes 4 servings

INGREDIENTS

2 pounds mixed heirloom tomatoes, sliced

1 tablespoon balsamic vinegar

2 teaspoons extra-virgin olive oil

Sea salt

¼ cup basil leaves or micro basil

8 tablespoons Cashew Chèvre (page 90)

Arrange the tomato slices on a large platter. Drizzle the tomatoes with the vinegar and oil and sprinkle with salt. Scatter the basil over the tomatoes. Drop the cheese by spoonfuls over the salad and serve.

EACH SERVING *194 calories (kcal) • 14 g fat • 0 mg cholesterol 16 g carbohydrates • 3 g dietary fiber • 5 g protein • 69 mg sodium 1,276 IU vitamin A • 48 mg vitamin C • 24 mg calcium • 2 mg iron*

CASHEW CHÈVRE

Enjoy this creamy vegan cheese on crackers or dolloped on the Ranch Caprese (page 89). The cashews must be soaked overnight before you can prepare the chèvre.

Makes about 1¼ cups

INGREDIENTS

1½ cups raw cashews

1 tablespoon extra-virgin olive oil

1 garlic clove

¼ teaspoon grated lemon zest

1½ teaspoons fresh lemon juice

½ teaspoon fresh thyme leaves

¼ teaspoon fresh rosemary leaves

¼ teaspoon sea salt

In a medium bowl, combine the cashews with enough water to cover by 3 inches and soak overnight.

Drain the cashews, reserving ½ cup of their soaking liquid. In a blender, combine the cashews, oil, garlic, lemon zest and juice, thyme, rosemary, and salt. Add ¼ cup of the reserved soaking liquid and blend until a smooth, thick puree forms, adding additional soaking liquid if necessary.

Transfer the puree to a small bowl and cover with plastic wrap. Refrigerate the cheese overnight to thicken slightly. (The cheese can be prepared up to 1 week ahead and refrigerated.)

EACH 2-TABLESPOON SERVING *131 calories (kcal) • 11 g fat • 0 mg cholesterol 7 g carbohydrates • 1 g dietary fiber • 3 g protein • 51 mg sodium 3 IU vitamin A • 1 mg vitamin C • 10 mg calcium • 1 mg iron*

RED QUINOA WITH BEETS AND RADICCHIO

This ruby- and russet-colored salad employs red quinoa, beets, and radicchio to create its rich hue.

Makes 6 servings

INGREDIENTS

8 medium (2- to 3-inch-diameter) beets

2 tablespoons extra-virgin olive oil, plus more for drizzling

1½ cups red quinoa, rinsed and drained

1 teaspoon sea salt, plus more to taste

¼ cup unsweetened pure cherry or pomegranate juice

3 tablespoons red wine vinegar

2 tablespoons walnut oil

⅓ cup finely chopped shallot

1 small head radicchio, torn into bite-size pieces

¼ cup dried sour cherries, chopped

Freshly ground black pepper

½ cup walnuts, toasted and chopped

Preheat the oven to 375°F. Arrange the beets in a small baking dish, add a drizzle of olive oil, and cover with foil. Roast the beets until tender when pierced with a small sharp knife, about 1 hour. Set aside to cool. (The roasted beets can be prepared up to 3 days ahead and stored in the refrigerator.)

In a heavy medium saucepan over medium-high heat, combine 3 cups water, the quinoa, and ½ teaspoon of the salt and bring to a boil. Reduce the heat and simmer until the liquid is reduced by half, about 10 minutes. Reduce the heat to low, cover, and cook until the quinoa is tender and the water has been absorbed, about 10 minutes longer. Transfer the quinoa to a large bowl and let cool to room temperature.

In small bowl, whisk together the cherry juice, vinegar, walnut oil, and olive oil to blend. Stir in the shallot and remaining ½ teaspoon salt.

Pour the dressing over the quinoa and toss to blend. Peel, halve, and thinly slice the beets. Add the beets, radicchio, and dried cherries to the quinoa and stir gently to combine. Season the salad with salt and pepper, sprinkle with the walnuts, and serve. (The salad can be prepared up to 2 days ahead. Cover and refrigerate; garnish with the toasted walnuts just before serving.)

EACH SERVING *382 calories (kcal) • 18 g fat • 0 mg cholesterol
48 g carbohydrates • 7 g dietary fiber • 11 g protein • 408 mg sodium
167 IU vitamin A • 6 mg vitamin C • 52 mg calcium • 1 mg iron*

QUINOA SALAD WITH SPRING VEGETABLES AND HERBS

This lemony quinoa salad features the best of spring—asparagus, snap peas, radishes, mint, dill, green onion, and green garlic, which is mild, tender young garlic.

Makes 4 to 6 servings

INGREDIENTS

1 cup quinoa, rinsed and drained

1 teaspoon sea salt

1 bunch asparagus (about 1 pound)

2 cups sugar snap or snow peas, trimmed and thinly sliced on an angle

1 bunch radishes, trimmed and sliced (reserve tops for garnish)

¼ cup loosely packed fresh mint leaves

1 scallion, thinly sliced

2 tablespoons coarsely chopped fresh dill

1 tablespoon minced green (spring) garlic, or 1 garlic clove, minced

2 tablespoons extra-virgin olive oil

½ teaspoon lemon zest

2 tablespoons fresh lemon juice

1 cup radish tops or wild arugula leaves, for garnish

Lemon wedges, for garnish

Nasturtium flowers and leaves, for garnish (optional; see Note)

In a heavy medium saucepan, bring 2 cups water, the quinoa, and ½ teaspoon of the salt to a boil over medium-high heat; reduce the heat and simmer until the liquid has reduced by half, about 10 minutes. Reduce the heat to low, cover, and cook until the quinoa is tender and the water has been absorbed, about 10 minutes longer. Transfer the quinoa to a large bowl and let stand until cooled to room temperature.

Fill a large skillet with 1 inch of salted water and bring to a simmer over high heat. Add the asparagus, cover, and cook until crisp-tender, about 2 minutes. Using tongs, transfer the asparagus to a bowl of ice water to cool. Drain the asparagus and pat dry with a clean kitchen towel. Cut the asparagus on an angle into 1-inch pieces and add to the quinoa along with the peas, radishes, mint, scallion, dill, and garlic.

In a small bowl, whisk together the olive oil, lemon zest and juice, and remaining ½ teaspoon salt to blend. Pour the dressing over the salad and stir to combine. (The salad can be prepared up to 1 day ahead. Cover and refrigerate.)

To serve, spoon the salad onto plates and garnish with the radish tops, lemon wedges, and nasturtiums, if using.

EACH SERVING *288 calories (kcal) • 11 g fat • 0 mg cholesterol*
38 g carbohydrates • 14 g dietary fiber • 10 g protein • 507 mg sodium
1,306 IU vitamin A • 42 mg vitamin C • 70 mg calcium • 5 mg iron

INGREDIENT NOTE *Nasturtium leaves and blossoms have a spicy flavor and the blossoms in particular take on a chive- or onion-like taste; smarten your salads with the petals and leaves.*

WARM BRUSSELS SPROUT CAESAR

The classic Caesar tosses Romaine lettuce with a dressing that includes anchovies, egg, and Worcestershire sauce. Here a vegan variation uses capers and organic soy sauce to reach the same umami—the fifth, "meaty-savory" taste—when tossed with thinly sliced and lightly sautéed Brussels sprouts.

Makes 4 servings

INGREDIENTS

For the Vegan Caesar Dressing

¼ cup extra-virgin olive oil

½ teaspoon lemon zest

2 tablespoons fresh lemon juice

1 large garlic clove

1 heaping teaspoon Dijon mustard

1 teaspoon soy sauce

1 tablespoon capers

Sea salt and freshly ground black pepper

For the Brussels Sprouts

1 pound Brussels sprouts

2 teaspoons extra-virgin olive oil

Chopped fresh flat-leaf parsley leaves, for garnish (optional)

Freshly ground black pepper, for serving

Make the Vegan Caesar dressing: In a blender, combine the oil, lemon zest and juice, garlic, mustard, and soy sauce and blend until the garlic is finely minced. Add the capers and pulse until the capers are chopped. Season the dressing to taste with salt and pepper. (The dressing can be made up to 4 days ahead. Cover and refrigerate.)

Make the Brussels Sprouts: Cut the Brussels sprouts in half from the top to the stem end, then thinly slice them crosswise. Heat the oil in a heavy large skillet over medium-high heat. Add the sliced Brussels sprouts and sauté until heated through and just beginning to wilt, about 4 minutes.

Transfer the Brussels sprouts to a large bowl. Add about 4 tablespoons dressing, and toss well. Garnish with parsley, if desired, and finish with freshly ground black pepper.

EACH SERVING *130 calories (kcal) • 10 g fat • 0 mg cholesterol
10 g carbohydrates • 4 g dietary fiber • 4 g protein • 112 mg sodium
771 IU vitamin A • 89 mg vitamin C • 45 mg calcium • 2 mg iron*

ASIAN SLAW WITH SPICY PEANUT DRESSING

Savory, spicy, sweet, and sour, this Thai-style slaw is tossed with a peanut dressing that everyone loves. Green papaya is an unripened, firm, green, and not-at-all-sweet version of enzyme-rich Mexican papaya. Look for it at Thai or Filipino markets. Don't worry if it's not available near you—the slaw is great made with green cabbage, too.

Makes 6 servings

INGREDIENTS

¼ cup fresh lime juice

3 tablespoons creamy peanut butter, such as Santa Cruz Organics

2 tablespoons tamari or soy sauce

1 tablespoon raw agave nectar

2 garlic cloves, crushed with a garlic press

2 teaspoons Sriracha sauce

4 cups peeled, shredded green papaya (from about one-half 5-pound papaya) or very thinly sliced green cabbage

¼ head (about 2 cups) very thinly sliced red cabbage

2 medium carrots, peeled and grated

1 red bell pepper, stemmed, seeded, and cut into very thin strips

2 scallions, thinly sliced

⅓ cup chopped fresh cilantro leaves

Sea salt

In a small bowl, whisk together the lime juice, peanut butter, tamari, agave nectar, garlic, and Sriracha to blend to create the dressing.

In a large bowl, combine the papaya, red cabbage, carrots, red pepper, scallions, and cilantro. Add the dressing and toss to coat. Season with salt. (The salad can be prepared several hours ahead. Cover and refrigerate.)

EACH SERVING *130 calories (kcal) • 4 g fat • 0 mg cholesterol 22 g carbohydrates • 4 g dietary fiber • 4 g protein • 415 mg sodium 4,810 IU vitamin A • 98 mg vitamin C • 54 mg calcium • 1 mg iron*

HIJIKI SALAD WITH PUMPKIN AND TAMARI SAUCE

One of the sea vegetables that is regularly enjoyed in Japan, hijiki is less well known outside Asia. Similar to arame, it is formed from dense strands of branch-like fronds and it's full of minerals. If you shy away from seaweed because of its fishy taste, you'll be surprised by this subtly flavored salad. Hijiki is incredibly absorbent, which is why it's essential to only eat hijiki that's been gathered wild, from the cleanest ocean waters, or hijiki that's certified organic. Mirin is a sweet rice wine with low alcohol content used in Japanese cooking. Organic mirin can be found in the Asian section of supermarkets or at Japanese markets.

Makes 4 side-dish servings

INGREDIENTS

1 cup dried hijiki, such as Eden Foods

3 tablespoons tamari

2 tablespoons mirin

2 tablespoons tahini (sesame seed paste)

1 tablespoon honey

½ cup soft tofu

½ cup very finely grated pumpkin, kabocha, or butternut squash (see Tip)

Soak the hijiki in 2 cups water for 10 minutes, but no longer (see Tip). Drain the hijiki, reserving the soaking water for another use, and transfer to a pot. Add fresh cold water to almost cover, and then bring to a boil over medium-high heat. Cover the pot, reduce the heat to low, and simmer for about 40 minutes. Add the tamari and continue to simmer, uncovered, for about 10 minutes, or until the liquid has totally evaporated.

Meanwhile, in a medium bowl, combine the mirin, tahini, and honey. Add the tofu and mash it with a fork, then mix to form a creamy dressing. Add the grated pumpkin and mix. Add the hijiki and mix until well combined. Serve the salad at room temperature.

EACH SERVING *125 calories (kcal) • 5 g fat • 0 mg cholesterol
13 g carbohydrates • 4 g dietary fiber • 5 g protein • 788 mg sodium
1,239 IU vitamin A • 2 mg vitamin C • 100 mg calcium • 2 mg iron*

COOK'S TIP *To finely grate the pumpkin, peel it then grate with a Microplane grater or other acid-etched superfine grating or shaving tool.*

COOK'S TIP *Soak sea vegetables just long enough to reconstitute their texture. Longer soaking just leaches out the minerals. We recommend using fresh water to simmer the hijiki; the reserved soaking water will keep, refrigerated, for about a week.*

VARIATIONS *For a spicier salad, add a little minced ginger and garlic or some sautéed onion; for a crunchy texture, add sliced fresh Asian mushrooms or finely sliced lotus root. For a richer tamari flavor, add more tamari to taste to the finished salad; top with finely chopped scallions.*

WHITE BEAN SALAD WITH OLIVES AND ARUGULA

Wild arugula grows in The Ranch's garden—it's pretty and adds peppery green zing to this colorful mix. This salad can be composed (as shown) with salad dressing served on the side, or tossed.

Makes 6 servings

INGREDIENTS

3 tablespoons extra-virgin olive oil

3 tablespoons sesame oil

3 tablespoons fresh lemon juice

3 tablespoons sherry wine vinegar

¼ teaspoon sea salt

2 (15-ounce) cans cannellini beans, drained and rinsed

2 carrots, peeled and sliced

1 red bell pepper, stemmed, seeded, and diced

½ small red onion, chopped

¾ cup pitted Kalamata olives, chopped

3 tablespoons chopped fresh basil

3 cups wild arugula leaves

1 cup cherry tomatoes, halved

⅓ cup toasted sesame seeds

Salt and freshly ground black pepper

Whisk together the olive and sesame oils, lemon juice, vinegar, and salt in a large bowl to blend. Add the beans, carrots, bell pepper, onion, olives, and basil and toss until coated. (Salad can be prepared up to 6 hours ahead; cover and refrigerate.)

Before serving, toss in the arugula, tomatoes, and sesame seeds. Season the salad to taste with salt and pepper.

EACH SERVING *287 calories (kcal) • 20 g fat • 0 mg cholesterol*
23 g carbohydrates • 7 g dietary fiber • 7 g protein • 224 mg sodium
3,963 IU vitamin A • 24 mg vitamin C • 83 mg calcium • 3 mg iron

COLLARD GREENS, SPROUTS, AND GOJI BERRY SALAD

Kale salad is a beloved staple, but if you want to add variety to your winter greens, look no further than the humble collard. Most commonly served slow-stewed, collards are also delicious eaten raw. Like kale, their tough texture can be softened without heat. And the health (and flavor) benefits of eating them raw as opposed to stewed are considerable. Vitamin C is destroyed by heat and vitamin A is only soluble in oil, not water, so massaging the collards in hemp oil, as we do in this salad recipe, means you'll get your vitamin A and C, too. There's more vitamin C in the goji berries to complement the dose from the collards; their gently sweet flavor is a perfect foil for the deep green earthy leaves and nutty sprouts. Sprouted seeds are available in health food stores.

Makes 6 side-dish servings

INGREDIENTS

6 large collard green leaves

1 tablespoon hemp oil, olive oil, or almond oil, plus more for massaging the collard greens

2 cups large sunflower seed sprouts

¾ cup dried goji berries (see Note, page 51)

1 medium orange (see Note)

2 teaspoons green powder, such as chlorella or spirulina

Sea salt and freshly ground black pepper

Stack the collard greens and roll them lengthwise into a tight cylinder; cut the roll crosswise into ⅛-inch-wide strips. Place the strips in a medium bowl. Pour a very small amount of hemp oil into the palm of your hand and rub your hands together to coat them. Scrunch the leaves to macerate them. Do this until the collard greens are slightly wilted.

Add the sprouts and goji berries to the collard greens and combine. Grate the zest from the orange and add to the collard green mixture.

Juice the orange over a small bowl. Whisk in the 1 tablespoon hemp oil and green powder and season with salt and pepper. Drizzle the dressing over the salad and serve.

EACH SERVING *147 calories (kcal) • 4 g fat • 0 mg cholesterol 22 g carbohydrates • 4 g dietary fiber • 6 g protein • 86 mg sodium 77 mg calcium • 6 mg iron • 5,193 IU vitamin A • 31 mg vitamin C*

INGREDIENT NOTE *Oranges contain 170 different antioxidant compounds, many of which are found in the skin and pith. The juice is sweet and loaded with nutritional benefits, too, so we decided to include both in this recipe.*

VARIATIONS *This recipe is infinitely adaptable. Try lime and lemon instead of oranges and any kind of dried berries, from cranberries to açaí.*

CURRIED CAULIFLOWER AND WARM SPELT SALAD

We're hard-pressed to think of a better flavor combination than cauliflower and cumin. The cauliflower sweetens and caramelizes as it slow roasts, and the cumin's oils absorb into the vegetable's flesh, where they are subtly enhanced by the turmeric and salt. For comfort and sustenance, we've added a bed of nutty spelt berries. The curried cauliflower on top is substantial; you can carve this vegan entrée at the table like a roasted chicken (minus the meat).

Makes 6 servings

INGREDIENTS

1½ cups spelt (see Note)

1 tablespoon extra-virgin olive oil

1½ tablespoons ground cumin

1½ tablespoons ground turmeric

1 tablespoon sea salt, plus more to taste

1 teaspoon crushed black peppercorns, plus more to taste

1 large head cauliflower

1 lime

1 tablespoon unrefined virgin coconut oil

2 shallots, finely chopped

4 garlic cloves, crushed

¼ cup unfiltered apple cider vinegar

1 tablespoon honey

½ cup chopped fresh cilantro leaves

Preheat the oven to 400°F.

In a medium bowl, soak the spelt in enough cold water to cover. In a small bowl, mix the olive oil with the cumin, turmeric, salt, and pepper to create a paste.

Using a sharp knife, trim the base of the cauliflower so that it's even and will stand up on its own. Remove any outer leaves that don't look fresh, but keep as many outer leaves as possible.

Place the cauliflower on a rimmed baking sheet. Using a pastry brush, paint the whole head of cauliflower with the spice paste, including the outer leaves. If you have any leftover paste, simply pour it over the cauliflower. Zest the lime over the cauliflower, then cut the lime in half and squeeze the juice over it. Bake the cauliflower until tender and golden brown, about 1 hour.

Meanwhile, drain the spelt and place it in a saucepan with 4½ cups water. Bring to a boil over high heat, then reduce the heat to maintain a simmer. Cover and continue to simmer the spelt until tender, about 50 minutes. Remove the spelt from the heat and keep warm.

Melt the coconut oil in a heavy small skillet over medium-low heat. Add the shallots and garlic and sauté until almost tender, about 3 minutes. Season with additional salt and crushed black pepper, stirring with a wooden spoon. Cover the skillet and reduce the heat to low. Cook until the shallots are very tender, about 3 minutes more.

In a cup, mix together the vinegar, honey, and cilantro to make a dressing. Pour the dressing over the spelt, then add the sautéed shallots and garlic and stir well to combine.

Arrange the warm spelt salad on a platter, place the curried cauliflower in the center, and carve and serve at the table.

EACH SERVING *200 calories (kcal)* • *6 g fat* • *0 mg cholesterol*
33 g carbohydrates • *5 g dietary fiber* • *7 g protein* • *502 mg sodium*
103 IU vitamin A • *51 mg vitamin C* • *45 mg calcium* • *2 mg iron*

INGREDIENT NOTE *The moist spelt berries in this dish do contain gluten, but at far lower levels than modern wheat. Celiacs or those eschewing all gluten can replace the spelt with a gluten-free grain such as quinoa or millet, but for people looking for a whole grain with a more balanced gluten content than modern wheat, spelt is a wonderful alternative.*

THE RANCH DETOX SALAD

The number one reason guests come to The Ranch is to detox: Detoxing their bodies from foods that are harmful; detoxing their minds from too much time spent in front of digital devices; detoxing their souls from all the demands that modern life makes on them. This salad delivers on its name, packing a powerful blend of cruciferous vegetables alongside leafy spinach and cleansing carrots. To enjoy the antioxidants and other phytonutrients that naturally occur in broccoli and spinach, it's essential to eat them very fresh. Cauliflower retains its full complement of nutrients for a week after picking if it's refrigerated, but broccoli and spinach are best eaten within two to three days of being harvested. You'll want spinach in a bunch rather than bagged baby spinach, as mature leaves contain far more phytonutrients than the baby ones.

Makes 6 appetizer or side-dish servings

INGREDIENTS

1 head broccoli, cut into florets, stem reserved

1 head cauliflower, cored and cut into florets

2 medium carrots, unpeeled, coarsely grated

4 large kale leaves, stems removed, finely chopped

2 cups finely chopped spinach leaves

2 tablespoons sunflower seeds

2 tablespoons raw pepitas

2 tablespoons cranberries, fresh if in season or dried

Purple Dressing (page 115)

Peel the broccoli stem and chop, then chop the broccoli and cauliflower florets with a sharp knife or by pulsing in a food processor. Place the chopped broccoli and cauliflower in a large bowl. Add the carrots, kale, and spinach and mix well.

Garnish the salad with the sunflower seeds, pepitas, and cranberries. Serve with Purple Dressing.

EACH SERVING WITH DRESSING *112 calories (kcal) • 8 g fat • 0 mg cholesterol 8 g carbohydrates • 3 g dietary fiber • 3 g protein • 152 mg sodium • 4,622 IU vitamin A 37 mg vitamin C • 37 mg calcium • 1 mg iron*

KALE AND CHICKPEA SALAD WITH PICKLED RED ONIONS

Kale is the most nutritious member of the cabbage family. It strengthens the blood, alkalinizes the whole body, and is rich in a group of phytonutrients called glucosinolates, which can offer protective qualities against some cancers. The most nutritious varieties are the red ones, including the Red Russian kale featured in this salad. Here, we pair it with the rich and earthy flavor of canned chickpeas; it may seem counterintuitive, but the high-pressure cooking process makes canned chickpeas softer than home-cooked ones, and makes their nutrients more bio-available. We finish the dish with Pickled Red Onions, which are as simple to make as they are delicious.

Makes 4 servings

INGREDIENTS

For the Sherry Vinaigrette

2 tablespoons sherry vinegar

Juice of 1 lemon

2 tablespoons sesame oil, plus more for massaging the kale

2 tablespoons extra-virgin olive oil

Sea salt

½ cup Pickled Red Onions (recipe opposite), chopped

1 pint cherry tomatoes, halved

¼ cup fresh basil leaves, finely chopped

1 cup pitted green olives, chopped

⅓ cup sesame seeds, toasted

1 bunch Red Russian kale

2 medium carrots, unpeeled, finely diced

1 medium red onion, peeled and finely diced

1 medium red bell pepper, stemmed, seeded, and finely diced

1 (14½-ounce) can chickpeas, drained and rinsed

In a medium nonreactive bowl, mix the vinegar, lemon juice, and sesame and olive oils with a fork to blend. Taste and season with salt as needed. Stir in the pickled onions, tomatoes, basil, olives, and sesame seeds and set aside.

On a chopping board, cut out the hard central stems from the kale. (These are great eaten as a snack with dip.) Tear or chop the kale leaves into a large bowl. Pour a very small amount of sesame oil into the palm of your hand and rub your hands together to coat them. You're now ready to massage the leaves, scrunching them forcefully to macerate them. Do this for about a minute, or until the kale is about half its original volume.

Divide the kale among plates or bowls and top with the carrots, diced red onion, red pepper, and chickpeas. Add the vinaigrette with pickled onion to the salad and serve.

EACH SERVING *464 calories (kcal) • 28 g fat • 0 mg cholesterol 49 g carbohydrates • 10 g dietary fiber • 10 g protein • 753 mg sodium 7,498 IU vitamin A • 75 mg vitamin C • 122 mg calcium • 3 mg iron*

PICKLED RED ONIONS

Makes 1 cup

INGREDIENTS

1 cup red wine vinegar

2 tablespoons raw agave nectar or maple syrup

2 cloves garlic, crushed

2 bay leaves

½ teaspoon peppercorns

1 large red onion, halved and thinly sliced

In a small saucepan combine ½ cup water, the vinegar, agave, garlic, bay leaves, and peppercorns. Bring to a boil, then reduce heat to a simmer. Add the onions and simmer for five minutes. Remove from the heat and pour into a nonreactive bowl; cool. Keep refrigerated in an airtight container for up to a month.

PER 2-TABLESPOON SERVING *48 calories (kcal) • 0 g fat • 0 mg cholesterol 12 g carbohydrates • 1 g dietary fiber • 1 g protein • 2 mg sodium 6 IU vitamin A • 3 mg vitamin C • 13 mg calcium • 0 mg iron*

SALAD DRESSINGS

Salad dressings are a crucial part of every vegetarian's arsenal. However fresh the greens, nothing can make or break a salad like the sauce that's used to dress it.

THE RANCH BALSAMIC VINAIGRETTE

A classic balsamic vinaigrette is simply balsamic vinegar mixed with olive oil, but we decided to play with this theme and came up with a light and flavorful version that doesn't contain any oil. The orange juice not only adds sweetness, but also a silky texture that's enhanced by the mustard, and the apple cider vinegar melds all of these flavors into one. Irresistibly fresh and delicate, we hope it will encourage you and your family to take extra servings of fresh salad greens.

Makes enough to dress 4 salad servings

INGREDIENTS

⅓ cup balsamic vinegar

¼ cup unfiltered apple cider vinegar (see Note)

2 tablespoons fresh orange juice

2 teaspoons coarse-grain mustard

In a small nonreactive bowl, whisk together both types of vinegar, the orange juice, 1 tablespoon water, and the mustard with a fork to blend. Pour over salad greens and toss to combine.

EACH 1-TABLESPOON SERVING *27 calories (kcal) • 0 g fat 0 mg cholesterol • 6 g carbohydrates • 0 g dietary fiber • 0 g protein 67 mg sodium • 0 IU vitamin A • 0 mg vitamin C • 0 mg calcium • 0 mg iron*

INGREDIENT NOTE *Apple cider vinegar is one of nature's greatest healing foods. All fermented foods contain a live culture that can replenish our own internal cultures, but apple cider vinegar also creates the perfect internal environment for your flora to flourish. For maximum benefit, choose unfiltered apple cider vinegar and shake the bottle before pouring. That way, the natural sediment will be distributed throughout the dressing and enhance its healthiness.*

COOK'S TIP *To make this dressing ahead, combine all the ingredients in a clean mason jar and screw on the lid. Shake to combine. The dressing can be refrigerated for up to 1 month. Before serving, simply shake to blend.*

THE RANCH CREAMY CHIVE AND DILL DRESSING

It's fun to re-create dairy foods with nondairy ingredients. Cheese, cream, and milk can all be mimicked using cashew nuts, bringing the satisfaction of a dairy-like texture, but without the lactose intolerance or other potential health disadvantages associated with pasteurized, processed dairy foods. Cashews contain unsaturated healthy fats, but as The Ranch is a calorie-reduced program, we serve only small portions of cashew-based foods to our guests. Thankfully a little goes a long way in a mock cream dressing recipe, so you can enjoy a silky textured sauce with a very small amount of nuts being included.

Makes enough to dress 20 salad servings

INGREDIENTS

1 cup cashews, soaked in water to cover overnight and drained

Juice of 1 lemon

1 pitted date

1 tablespoon minced fresh chives

1 teaspoon minced fresh dill

In a blender, combine the cashews, lemon juice, and date. Add a little water and blend on high speed. Little by little, add more water, up to ¼ cup total, until a creamy, pourable consistency is achieved. Transfer the dressing to a small bowl, stir in the chives and dill, and serve immediately over greens.

EACH 1-TABLESPOON SERVING *68 calories (kcal) • 5 g fat • 0 mg cholesterol 4 g carbohydrates • 1 g dietary fiber • 2 g protein • 2 mg sodium • 12 IU vitamin A 1 mg vitamin C • 6 mg calcium • 1 mg iron*

LEMON-DILL VINAIGRETTE

This simple and brightly flavored dressing is tart, herbal, and tasty on steamed carrots and cauliflower or grilled fish. Chervil, cilantro, and tarragon make a savory substitution for the dill.

Makes enough to dress 12 salad servings

INGREDIENTS

5 tablespoons extra-virgin olive oil

½ teaspoon lemon zest

3 tablespoons lemon juice

2 tablespoons rice vinegar

½ teaspoon sea salt

3 tablespoons chopped fresh dill

In a small bowl, whisk the olive oil, lemon zest and juice, vinegar, and salt to blend. (Dressing can be made ahead. Cover and let stand at cool room temperature for up to 8 hours.) Add the dill and stir until the dressing is blended.

EACH 1-TABLESPOON SERVING *53 calories (kcal) • 6 g fat • 0 mg cholesterol 0 g carbohydrates • 0 g dietary fiber • 0 g protein • 117 mg sodium 11 IU vitamin A • 2 mg vitamin C • 1 mg calcium • 0 mg iron*

ORANGE AND TAHINI CILANTRO DRESSING

This simple dressing complements winter greens perfectly. The orange adds a welcome sweetness to counter the bitterness of more hardy greens, like raw kale and Brussels sprouts. The olive oil softens these winter vegetables, making their texture deliciously crisp instead of distractingly dense.

Makes enough to dress 8 salad servings

INGREDIENTS

Zest of 1 orange

Juice of 3 oranges (about 1 cup)

2 tablespoons tahini (sesame seed paste)

½ cup extra-virgin olive oil

⅓ cup finely chopped fresh cilantro leaves

1 teaspoon finely ground pink Himalayan salt

In a small bowl, combine the orange zest and juice, tahini, oil, cilantro, and salt and whisk with a fork to blend. Pour over salad greens and toss to combine. (The dressing can be stored in the refrigerator for up to 1 week.)

EACH 1-TABLESPOON SERVING *41 calories (kcal) • 4 g fat • 0 mg cholesterol*
1 g carbohydrates • 0 g dietary fiber • 0 g protein • 60 mg sodium
12 IU vitamin A • 0 mg vitamin C • 2 mg calcium • 0 mg iron

PURPLE DRESSING

Tart and summery, this juicy oil-free dressing is perfect for drizzling over a summer mesclun salad, or as a light sauce to dress steamed grains. It contains maca, a Peruvian superfood believed to support endocrine function, sexual health, and physical endurance. For our guests, maca is a source of stamina that we add to their daily smoothies. It's not the most delicious ingredient in our kitchen, so it's best to add it to strongly flavored recipes, such as this tasty blueberry dressing. Toasting the maca sweetens the alkaloid flavors and improves its nutritional profile, paving the way for better absorption of phytonutrients.

Makes enough to lightly dress 4 to 6 salad servings

INGREDIENTS

1 cup fresh or frozen blueberries

Zest and juice of 1 lemon

1 tablespoon maca powder

Sea salt and freshly ground black pepper to taste

In a blender, combine the blueberries and lemon zest and juice on high speed until liquified.

In a small dry skillet over a high heat, toast the maca, stirring continuously, for about 30 seconds. Add the toasted maca to the blueberries and combine. Season with salt and pepper. Use the dressing immediately.

EACH 1-TABLESPOON SERVING *26 calories (kcal) • 0 g fat*
0 mg cholesterol • 6 g carbohydrates • 1 g dietary fiber • 0 g protein
5 mg sodium • 21 IU vitamin A • 7 mg vitamin C • 4 mg calcium • 0 mg iron

hearty mains

KOREAN KELP NOODLES WITH NAPA CABBAGE AND ASIAN PEARS

The most mineral-rich ingredients that can be found are sea vegetables such as kelp noodles. They absorb flavors, so you can simply marinate them to create an exciting entrée.

Makes 4 servings

INGREDIENTS

2 cups rice vinegar

1 cup shoyu

1½ pounds kelp noodles, thoroughly washed

1 cup arame

2 tablespoons toasted sesame oil

4 garlic cloves, crushed with a garlic press

2 tablespoons crushed red pepper flakes

4 scallions, trimmed and finely chopped

½ pound sunflower sprouts, washed, dried, and separated

4 cups finely shredded Napa cabbage (about ½ head)

2 Asian pears (see Note), cored and finely diced

½ pound enoki mushrooms, broken into individual strands

Zest and juice of 2 limes

¼ cup sesame seeds

In a large nonreactive bowl, combine the vinegar and shoyu. Add the kelp noodles, separating the strands with your fingers. (If necessary, use a plate to keep the noodles submerged.) Let marinate for at least 30 minutes (see Tip).

When you're ready to proceed, use tongs to transfer the kelp noodles to a serving platter. Place the arame in the marinade and soak for 10 minutes. In a frying pan, heat the sesame oil over low heat. Add the garlic, red pepper flakes, scallions, sprouts, cabbage, pears, mushrooms, and lime zest and sauté for 3 to 5 minutes. Add ¼ cup of the reserved marinade along with the arame and cover the pan. Cook until the vegetables are wilted and fragrant, about 3 minutes more. Add the lime juice and sesame seeds and stir to combine.

Top the kelp noodles with the sautéed vegetables and serve.

EACH SERVING *318 calories (kcal)* • *22 g fat* • *0 mg cholesterol*
28 g carbohydrates • *13 g dietary fiber* • *8 g protein* • *1,209 mg sodium*
1,965 IU vitamin A • *26 mg vitamin C* • *365 mg calcium* • *4 mg iron*

INGREDIENT NOTE *An Asian pear is a fruit with a texture that is very dense and watery, like a water chestnut.*

COOK'S TIP *Kelp noodles will become softer and more intensely flavored the longer they marinate. If time allows, leave them in the marinade overnight for use the next day.*

RISOTTO WITH MUSHROOMS, ROASTED KABOCHA SQUASH, AND PARSNIPS

This comforting winter risotto is technically a *farrotto*, as it employs the same cooking method but a different grain. The benefit of using farro is the wholesomeness and the robust nutty flavor of the grain.

Makes 4 to 6 servings

INGREDIENTS

10 ounces kabocha or butternut squash, peeled and cut into ½-inch dice (about 1½ cups)

2 parsnips, unpeeled, cut into ½-inch dice (about 1½ cups)

4 tablespoons extra-virgin olive oil

Sea salt and coarsely ground black pepper

6 fresh sage leaves, chopped

¼ cup minced shallot (about 1 large)

2 garlic cloves, minced

10 ounces cremini, maitake, or shiitake mushrooms, cut into ⅓-inch-thick slices

1 cup pearled farro

4 to 5 cups low-sodium vegetable broth

2 sprigs fresh thyme

¼ cup chopped fresh flat-leaf parsley, for serving

Preheat the oven to 400°F. On a large heavy baking sheet, toss the squash and parsnips with 2 tablespoons of the oil. Sprinkle with salt and pepper. Roast until the vegetables are golden brown in spots, stirring once, about 30 minutes. Sprinkle with the sage and let cool.

Heat the remaining 2 tablespoons oil in a large saucepan over medium heat. Add the shallots and garlic and sauté until soft, about 5 minutes. Increase the heat to medium-high. Add the mushrooms and sauté until browned, about 10 minutes. Add the farro and cook for 1 minute to toast, stirring frequently. Reduce the heat to medium-low. Add 1 cup of the broth and the thyme and cook until the broth has been absorbed, stirring frequently, about 5 minutes. Add the remaining broth, ½ cup at a time, allowing the broth to be absorbed before adding more, and continue cooking until the farro is tender, about 25 minutes. Remove the thyme sprigs. Stir in the roasted squash and parsnips, season with salt and pepper, and sprinkle with the chopped parsley.

EACH SERVING (BASED ON 6 SERVINGS) *362 calories (kcal) • 6 g fat 0 mg cholesterol • 74 g carbohydrates • 7 g dietary fiber • 11 g protein • 124 mg sodium 1,609 IU vitamin A • 19 mg vitamin C • 29 mg calcium • 4 mg iron*

FRAGRANT GREEN CURRY WITH THAI EGGPLANT

This Thai-style curry is made from a fresh puree of traditional green curry ingredients including lemongrass, chili pepper, and grated ginger, plus a purchased green curry paste. Thai eggplant are small, round, and green—you can find them, as well as the curry paste, lemongrass, Thai basil, and kaffir lime leaves, at a Thai market.

Makes 4 to 6 servings

INGREDIENTS

1 tablespoon grapeseed or olive oil

½ cup finely chopped shallots (about 2 large)

¼ cup finely chopped jalapeño (about 1 large)

¼ cup finely chopped lemongrass, or 2 tablespoons lemongrass paste

2 tablespoons grated peeled fresh ginger

4 garlic cloves, finely chopped

2 teaspoons Thai green curry paste

1 teaspoon ground coriander

1 teaspoon ground cumin

¼ cup chopped fresh basil leaves, preferably Thai basil

¼ cup finely chopped cilantro stems

1 (13.5-ounce) can light coconut milk

3 kaffir lime leaves

2 tablespoons tamari or soy sauce

1 tablespoon raw agave nectar

8 Thai eggplants (about 12 ounces), stemmed and quartered, or 3 small Japanese eggplants, cut in half lengthwise, then cut crosswise into 1½-inch pieces

½ head cauliflower, trimmed and cut into 1-inch florets (about 3 cups)

1½ cups sliced carrots, unpeeled

1 bell pepper, stemmed, seeded, and cut into ¾-inch pieces

Sea salt

Cilantro leaves, for garnish

Heat the oil in a heavy large saucepan over medium-high heat. Add the shallots, jalapeño, lemongrass, ginger, and garlic and sauté until tender, about 5 minutes. Add the curry paste, coriander, and cumin and stir until fragrant, about 2 minutes. Add the basil and the cilantro stems and cook until the herbs wilt. Stir in 1 cup water. Carefully transfer the curry mixture to the blender and puree until smooth.

Return the puree to the saucepan and add the coconut milk, lime leaves, tamari, and agave nectar, and bring to simmer. Add the eggplant, cauliflower, carrots, and bell pepper and simmer over medium heat until the vegetables are tender, about 20 minutes. Season with salt. Ladle the curry into bowls, sprinkle with cilantro, and serve. (The curry can be prepared up to 3 days ahead; cool, cover, and refrigerate.)

EACH SERVING (BASED ON 6 SERVINGS) *176 calories (kcal) • 6 g fat 0 mg cholesterol • 28 g carbohydrates • 8 g dietary fiber • 6 g protein • 405 mg sodium 5,697 IU vitamin A • 54 mg vitamin C • 45 mg calcium • 2 mg iron*

GRILLED ARTICHOKES WITH GARLIC BROTH AND WHITE BEAN BRANDADE

You can serve the delectable grilled artichokes with the fragrant broth for an appetizer or side dish, but when paired with the creamy brandade and a lemon-dressed arugula salad, you have a feast.

Makes 4 servings

INGREDIENTS

For the Brandade

1 tablespoon extra-virgin olive oil

1 medium onion, chopped

4 garlic cloves, chopped

2 (15-ounce) cans cannellini beans, drained and rinsed

2 teaspoons fresh rosemary leaves

½ teaspoon lemon zest

For the Artichokes and Garlic Broth

4 large artichokes with stems

¾ cup low-sodium vegetable broth

1 medium shallot, sliced

4 garlic cloves, thinly sliced

1 tablespoon white wine vinegar

½ teaspoon lemon zest

Extra-virgin olive oil, for brushing

2 tablespoons chopped fresh flat-leaf parsley leaves

2 teaspoons chopped fresh thyme

Lemon wedges, for serving

Make the Brandade: Heat the oil in a large heavy skillet over medium-high heat. Add the onion, cover, and cook until just tender, about 2 minutes. Uncover the pan, add the garlic, and sauté until the onion is golden brown, about 4 minutes. Stir in the beans, ⅔ cup water, the rosemary, and the lemon zest and simmer briefly to blend the flavors, about 2 minutes. Carefully transfer the white bean mixture to a food processor fitted with the metal blade and puree until smooth. (The brandade can be prepared up to 3 days ahead; cover and refrigerate.)

Make the Artichokes and Garlic Broth: With a sharp knife, trim ¼ inch from the artichoke stems. Pull off the tough outer leaves. Trim off the top 1½ inch from each artichoke; use kitchen scissors to snip off any sharp edges on the remaining leaves. In a large pot fitted with a steamer basket, steam the artichokes until just tender when pierced with a small, sharp knife, about 12 minutes. Using tongs, remove the artichokes from the steamer and let stand until cool enough to handle. Cut the artichokes lengthwise in half; remove the chokes.

In a small heavy saucepan, simmer the broth with the shallot, garlic, vinegar, and lemon zest over medium heat until the broth has reduced to ½ cup, about 3 minutes; reserve. (The broth and artichokes can be prepared up to 1 day ahead; cover separately and refrigerate.)

Preheat an outdoor grill to medium heat or a cast-iron grill pan over medium-high heat. Brush the artichokes lightly with olive oil. Grill the artichokes until golden brown, about 3 minutes per side; set aside.

Meanwhile, bring the garlic broth to a simmer. Return the white bean puree to a skillet and stir over medium until heated through. Divide the brandade among shallow bowls and top with the grilled artichokes. Spoon the broth over the artichokes and around the brandade. Sprinkle the parsley and thyme over the artichokes, garnish with the lemon wedges, and serve.

EACH SERVING *252 calories (kcal) • 5 g fat • 0 mg cholesterol*
43 g carbohydrates • 15 g dietary fiber • 13 g protein • 203 mg sodium
205 IU vitamin A • 24 mg vitamin C • 140 mg calcium • 4 mg iron

NETTLE AND BASIL PESTO WITH WALNUTS AND WHOLE-GRAIN PASTA

Young stinging nettle can be foraged on the grounds of The Ranch every spring. The wild herb is an excellent source of vitamins A and C, iron, potassium, calcium, and manganese, and it contains mineral salts. Wild nettles do indeed sting, but it's easy to remove the stinging chemicals in the plants by soaking them in cold water (only young nettle leaves should be used). Nettles can be purchased at farmers' markets in the spring. They possess a delightful spinach-meets-cucumber flavor.

Makes 4 servings

INGREDIENTS

1 cup tightly packed young nettle leaves (from about 1 bunch)

1 cup tightly packed fresh basil leaves

½ cup walnuts, toasted

2 garlic cloves

¼ cup extra-virgin olive oil

Sea salt and freshly ground black pepper

8 ounces gluten-free multigrain or whole wheat spaghetti

⅓ cup almond milk, homemade (page 44) or unsweetened store-bought

Soak the nettle leaves in water to cover for a minimum of 9 hours. Drain and pat dry.

In a food processor with the metal blade attached, process the nettle, basil, walnuts, and garlic until finely chopped. Add the oil and blend until a smooth paste forms. Season the pesto to taste with salt and pepper. (The pesto can be prepared up to 2 days ahead; transfer to an airtight container and refrigerate.)

In a large pot of rapidly boiling salted water, cook the pasta until tender but firm to the bite, about 7 minutes. Drain the pasta, reserving ¾ cup of the pasta cooking liquid.

Meanwhile, in a small heavy saucepan, bring the almond milk to a simmer over medium heat. Add the pesto and ½ cup of the reserved pasta cooking liquid and return to a simmer. Toss the pesto mixture with the pasta in a large, heated pasta bowl. Add the additional reserved pasta cooking liquid by the tablespoonful to moisten if necessary. Season the pasta to taste with salt and pepper and serve.

EACH SERVING *442 calories (kcal) • 25 g fat • 0 mg cholesterol
51 g carbohydrates • 6 g dietary fiber • 10 g protein • 14 mg sodium
1,055 IU vitamin A • 3 mg vitamin C • 155 mg calcium • 4 mg iron*

POLENTA WITH ROASTED ACORN SQUASH RAGOUT

Sage, onions, and cranberries accompany the squash atop creamy polenta—a perfect fall meal. Organically grown and stone-milled polenta is available from specialty mills and stores, and online.

Makes 4 servings

INGREDIENTS

For the Squash Ragout

1 acorn squash (about 1 to 1¼ pounds)

1 onion

1 tablespoon plus 1 teaspoon extra-virgin olive oil

Sea salt and freshly ground black pepper

4 garlic cloves, chopped

1 cup low-sodium vegetable broth

¼ cup dried cranberries

2 teaspoons sherry wine vinegar

1 teaspoon cornstarch

For the Polenta

1 tablespoon plus 2 teaspoons extra-virgin olive oil

1 garlic clove, crushed with a garlic press

½ teaspoon sea salt

1 cup stone-ground grits (polenta)

¼ cup fresh sage leaves, for garnish

Make the Squash Ragout: Preheat the oven to 400°F. With a sharp knife, cut the squash in half from stem to tip. Remove the seeds and cut each half into 6 slices. Cut the onion into 12 wedges from the root end to the tip. Coat a large heavy baking sheet with 1 tablespoon of the oil. Arrange the squash slices and onion wedges on the baking sheet in a single layer and sprinkle with salt and pepper. Roast in the oven until the vegetables are browned on the bottoms, about 10 minutes; turn and continue roasting until the squash and onion are browned on all sides and tender, about 10 minutes longer. Transfer the squash mixture to a bowl and keep warm.

Meanwhile, heat 1 teaspoon of the oil in small heavy saucepan over medium heat. Add the garlic and sauté until tender, about 1 minute. Add half of the broth, the cranberries, and the vinegar and simmer until the cranberries are softened, about 2 minutes. Whisk the cornstarch into the remaining broth; add the slurry to the cranberry mixture and cook until the sauce boils and thickens, about 1 minute.

Make the Polenta: In a heavy medium saucepan, bring 3½ cups water, 2 teaspoons of the oil, the garlic, and salt to a boil over medium-high heat. Gradually whisk in the grits (polenta). Reduce the heat to low and simmer, stirring frequently, until the polenta is tender and creamy, about 30 minutes. Keep the polenta warm.

Heat the remaining 1 tablespoon oil in a small heavy saucepan over medium-high heat. Add the sage leaves and fry until crisp, about 1 minute. Transfer to paper towels to drain.

Return the cranberry sauce to a simmer to reheat if necessary. Pour the sauce over the squash mixture and stir the ragout gently to combine.

Spoon the warm polenta into bowls and top with the ragout. Sprinkle with the fried sage leaves and serve.

EACH SERVING *344 calories (kcal) • 12 g fat • 0 mg cholesterol*
57 g carbohydrates • 5 g dietary fiber • 4 g protein • 281 mg sodium
492 IU vitamin A • 16 mg vitamin C • 72 mg calcium • 2 mg iron

INDIAN-SPICED SWISS CHARD ROLLS WITH COCONUT TOMATO SAUCE

Steamed, organically grown brown rice is available in the freezer section of many markets. It's a wonderful convenience for making healthy dishes like this one. You could also substitute quinoa for the brown rice, if you desire.

Makes 4 to 6 servings

INGREDIENTS

For the Coconut Tomato Sauce

2 tablespoons extra-virgin olive oil

½ cup chopped onion

2 garlic cloves, minced

2 teaspoons minced peeled fresh ginger

1 tablespoon mild curry powder

¼ cinnamon stick

1 (28-ounce) can crushed fire-roasted tomatoes

1 (13.5-ounce) can coconut milk

For the Swiss Chard Rolls

3 carrots, cut into ¼-inch dice (about 1½ cups)

1 tablespoon extra-virgin olive oil

½ teaspoon ground cumin

½ teaspoon garam masala

¼ teaspoon cayenne pepper

Sea salt and freshly ground black pepper

1 cup cooked brown rice

3 scallions, trimmed and sliced

¼ cup raisins

¼ cup sliced almonds

12 large rainbow Swiss chard leaves

Make the Coconut Tomato Sauce: Heat the oil in a heavy medium saucepan over medium heat. Add the onion, garlic, and ginger and sauté until the onion is tender, about 8 minutes. Stir in the curry powder and cinnamon stick and cook until fragrant, about 30 seconds. Stir in the tomatoes and coconut milk and simmer until the sauce thickens and has reduced to about 3 cups, about 20 minutes. (The sauce can be made up to 1 week ahead; cover and refrigerate.)

Make the Swiss Chard Rolls: Preheat the oven to 400°F. On a large heavy baking sheet, toss the carrots with the oil, cumin, garam masala, and cayenne, and then sprinkle with salt and black pepper. Roast the carrots until golden brown and tender, about 15 minutes; keep the oven on. Transfer to a medium bowl and stir in the rice, scallions, raisins, and almonds; season to taste with salt and black pepper. (The filling can be made up to 1 day ahead; cover and refrigerate.)

Bring a large skillet of water to a simmer. Using tongs, blanch the chard leaves in the simmering water, one at a time, until just tender. Transfer them to baking sheets lined with kitchen towels to cool. Using a small, sharp knife, remove the stem and large center rib from each leaf.

Divide the filling evenly among the chard leaves (about 3 tablespoons per leaf), mounding it slightly in the center of each leaf. Fold the sides of each leaf up and over the filling to enclose, and then roll up each leaf like a burrito.

Spoon half the sauce over the bottom of a 12-inch oval or 8-inch square baking dish. Arrange the chard rolls on top of the sauce, seam side down, and then top with the remaining sauce. (The rolls can be prepared up to 6 hours ahead; tightly cover the baking dish with plastic wrap and refrigerate.) Bake the rolls until heated through, about 20 minutes. Transfer 2 or 3 rolls with sauce to each plate and serve.

EACH SERVING (BASED ON 6 SERVINGS) *338 calories (kcal) • 23 g fat 0 mg cholesterol • 31 g carbohydrates • 6 g dietary fiber • 7 g protein • 554 mg sodium 5,693 IU vitamin A • 28 mg vitamin C • 61 mg calcium • 4 mg iron*

THAI LARB WITH CAULIFLOWER AND COCONUT RICE IN LETTUCE CUPS

Larb is a Thai dish of minced meat and aromatics. In our version, stir-fried brown rice makes an excellent stand-in for the meat, and by adding finely chopped cauliflower to the rice, we've reduced the carbs and added wonderful flavor and texture.

Makes 4 servings

INGREDIENTS

For the Ginger-Lime Sauce

6 tablespoons fresh lime juice

2 tablespoons tamari

2 tablespoons raw agave nectar

1 teaspoon minced peeled fresh ginger

For the Larb Filling

¼ head cauliflower, separated into florets

2 tablespoons peanut or vegetable oil

2½ teaspoons Thai red curry paste

¾ cup chopped shallots (about 3 large)

3 garlic cloves, minced

2 kaffir lime leaves, finely sliced (optional)

1 cup cooked brown rice

2 tablespoons grated unsweetened coconut

2 tablespoons canned unsweetened coconut milk

Sea salt and freshly ground black pepper

For the Lettuce Cups and Toppings

8 butter lettuce leaves or very large spinach leaves

2 scallions, trimmed and sliced

1 English (hothouse) cucumber, unpeeled, cut into matchsticks

2 carrots, unpeeled, cut into matchsticks

1 cup loosely packed fresh cilantro leaves

Make the Ginger-Lime Sauce: In a small bowl, mix the lime juice, tamari, agave nectar, and ginger to blend. Cover and set aside up to 4 hours.

Make the Larb Filling: Place the cauliflower in a food processor with the metal blade attached. Pulse until the cauliflower is chopped into small pieces resembling rice. (You should have about 1½ cups.)

In a large skillet over medium-high heat, heat the oil and stir in the curry paste. Add the shallots and sauté until golden, about 3 minutes. Add the cauliflower rice, garlic, and lime leaves and sauté until the cauliflower is just turning golden brown, about 1 minute. Mix in the brown rice, grated coconut, and coconut milk; stir-fry until the rice is heated through and the cauliflower is just tender, about 2 minutes. Season with salt and pepper.

Assemble the lettuce cups: Place two lettuce leaves on each serving plate. Fill each leaf with the rice and cauliflower larb and top with scallions, cucumber, carrots, and cilantro. Drizzle a little ginger-lime sauce over each cup and serve.

EACH SERVING *240 calories (kcal) • 10 g fat • 0 mg cholesterol*
37 g carbohydrates • 5 g dietary fiber • 6 g protein • 587 mg sodium
5,740 IU vitamin A • 41 mg vitamin C • 75 mg calcium • 2 mg iron

COLLARD GREEN SUSHI WITH CURRY-TAHINI DIPPING SAUCE

Makes 4 servings (16 pieces total)

INGREDIENTS

For the Curry-Tahini Dipping Sauce

⅓ cup tahini (sesame seed paste)

¼ cup fresh lemon juice

¼ cup minced fresh cilantro leaves

2 teaspoons curry powder

Sea salt and coarsely ground
black pepper

For the Collard Rolls

4 large green collard leaves

2 tablespoons unrefined virgin coconut oil

2 garlic cloves, minced

1 teaspoon orange zest

⅓ cup fresh orange juice

1 tablespoon coconut sugar (see page 199)

1 bunch curly kale (about 6 ounces),
stemmed and thinly sliced

Sea salt and freshly ground pepper

1 avocado, halved, pitted,
peeled, and thinly sliced

1 carrot, unpeeled, cut into matchsticks

½ English (hothouse) cucumber,
unpeeled, cut into matchsticks

1 cup alfalfa or broccoli sprouts

Make the Curry-Tahini Dipping Sauce: In a small bowl, whisk together the tahini, lemon juice, ¼ cup water, the cilantro, and curry powder to blend. Season to taste with salt and pepper.

Make the Collard Rolls: Fill a large skillet halfway with water and bring to a boil. Line a baking sheet with a kitchen towel. Using a sharp knife, trim the thick stems off the collard leaves and then trim off any raised portions of the remaining stems. This will leave you with flat leaves that are easy to roll up. Place 1 leaf in the boiling water. Blanch until softened, turning once, about 10 seconds. Remove with tongs, and spread the leaf out on the towel to drain. Repeat with the remaining collard leaves.

Heat the coconut oil in a large skillet over medium heat. Add the garlic and sauté for 30 seconds. Add the orange zest and juice and the coconut sugar and cook until the sugar dissolves, about 1 minute. Add the kale and sauté until the kale is tender and all the liquid has evaporated, about 5 minutes. Season to taste with salt and pepper. Cool completely.

On a work surface, spread out one of the collard leaves with its stem end facing you. Starting about 1 inch from the bottom of the leaf, spread about ¼ cup of the kale mixture on the leaf. Top the kale with one-quarter of the avocado, one-quarter each of the carrot and cucumber sticks, and ¼ cup of the sprouts. Starting at the stem end, roll the leaf up like a sushi roll to enclose the kale filling, keeping the roll tight. Repeat with the remaining collard leaves and filling. (The collard rolls can be made up to 2 hours ahead. Cover with a kitchen towel and let stand at room temperature.)

Using a sharp knife, trim off the ends of each roll, then cut each roll crosswise into 4 sushi pieces. Place the pieces cut-side up on a platter and serve, passing the dipping sauce separately.

EACH SERVING *324 calories (kcal)* • *25 g fat* • *0 mg cholesterol*
23 g carbohydrates • *8 g dietary fiber* • *11 g protein* • *336 mg sodium*
5,723 IU vitamin A • *60 mg vitamin C* • *163 mg calcium* • *4 mg iron*

EGGPLANT WRAPS WITH MUHAMARA AND TAHINI SAUCE

This hearty sandwich wrap is a perfect choice for a brown-bag or picnic lunch. Sprouted-grain tortillas are healthy and delicious, although not gluten-free. If you avoid gluten, substitute large brown rice tortillas or other gluten-free flatbread. The Middle Eastern condiments—a tahini sauce made with garlic and lemon juice, and muhamara, a red pepper spread—are excellent dips for crudité as well. To lower the calories and sodium, use 1½ tablespoons muhamara per serving instead of the 3 tablespoons called for in the recipe.

Makes 4 wraps

INGREDIENTS

For the Tahini Sauce

½ cup tahini (sesame seed paste)

3 tablespoons fresh lemon juice

1 garlic clove, crushed with a garlic press

½ teaspoon sea salt

For the Eggplant Wraps

1 large eggplant (about 1½ pounds), cut into ½-inch-thick rounds

2 tablespoons plus 2 teaspoons extra-virgin olive oil

2 teaspoons coarsely crushed cumin seeds

⅓ bunch spinach leaves, cut into thick ribbons (about 1 cup)

½ cup fresh mint leaves

½ cup chopped fresh cilantro leaves

1 teaspoon fresh lemon juice

¾ cup Gluten-Free Muhamara (page 136)

4 (9-inch) sprouted grain or brown rice tortillas

Make the Tahini Sauce: In a small bowl, stir together the tahini, lemon juice, ¼ cup water, the garlic, and the salt to blend. (The sauce can be prepared up to 1 week ahead; cover and refrigerate.)

Make the Eggplant Wraps: Preheat the broiler. On a large heavy baking sheet, arrange the eggplant slices in a single layer. Brush both sides of the eggplant slices with 2 tablespoons of the oil and sprinkle evenly with the cumin. Broil the eggplant until golden brown, about 5 minutes. Turn over the slices and continue to broil until the second sides are golden brown, about 4 minutes longer. (The eggplant can be prepared up to 1 day ahead; wrap the slices in plastic wrap and refrigerate.)

In a large bowl, combine the spinach, mint, and cilantro. Add the remaining 2 teaspoons oil and the lemon juice and toss to blend. Spread about 3 tablespoons muhamara down the center of each tortilla. Top with the eggplant slices, dividing them evenly among the tortillas. Spoon about 2 tablespoons of the tahini sauce over the eggplant layer on each wrap. Divide the spinach salad among the wraps. Fold one-half of a tortilla over the filling to enclose, and then roll up the tortilla. Repeat with the other wraps. (The wraps can be prepared up to 1 day ahead; wrap tightly in waxed paper and refrigerate.) Cut the wraps in half to serve.

GLUTEN-FREE MUHAMARA

Muhamara is a versatile Middle Eastern condiment made from roasted red peppers, walnuts, pomegranate molasses, and bread crumbs. This version uses quinoa flakes instead of bread to create a fabulous gluten-free dip or spread.

Makes about 1 cup

INGREDIENTS

1 (12-ounce) jar roasted
red bell peppers, drained

1 large garlic clove

⅓ cup walnuts, toasted

½ cup quinoa flakes

1 tablespoon extra-virgin olive oil

1 tablespoon pomegranate molasses

½ teaspoon sea salt

¼ teaspoon cayenne pepper

In a food processor with the metal blade attached, puree the roasted peppers and garlic until the garlic is very finely chopped. Add the walnuts and pulse until finely ground. Transfer the puree to a medium bowl and, with a spatula, mix in the quinoa flakes, oil, pomegranate molasses, salt, and cayenne pepper. (The muhamara can be prepared up to 4 days ahead; cover and refrigerate.)

EACH WRAP (WITH 3 TABLESPOONS MUHAMARA) *487 calories (kcal) • 26 g fat 0 mg cholesterol • 52 g carbohydrates • 10 g dietary fiber • 11 g protein • 770 mg sodium 11,865 IU vitamin A • 22 mg vitamin C • 130 mg calcium • 6 mg iron*

EACH WRAP (WITH 1½ TABLESPOONS MUHAMARA) *392 calories (kcal) • 20 g fat 0 mg cholesterol • 44 g carbohydrates • 9 g dietary fiber • 9 g protein • 543 mg sodium 11,505 IU vitamin A • 13 mg vitamin C • 110 mg calcium • 5 mg iron*

MUSTARD GREEN WRAPS WITH GARLICKY MILLET AND TOMATOES

Makes 4 servings

INGREDIENTS

1 cup millet

¼ teaspoon sea salt

½ cup unrefined virgin coconut oil, melted and cooled

1 large shallot, finely chopped

4 garlic cloves, crushed with a garlic press

30 cherry tomatoes, halved

12 capers, finely chopped

½ cup chopped fresh cilantro leaves

8 large mustard green leaves

Sea salt and freshly ground black pepper

In a medium saucepan, bring the millet, salt, and 2½ cups water to a boil over high heat, then reduce the heat and simmer, covered, for 15 minutes. Remove from the heat and leave to rest for 10 minutes.

While the millet is simmering, heat about 1 tablespoon of the coconut oil in another pan over medium heat until melted, then reduce the heat to low and add the shallot. Sauté for a few minutes, then add the garlic, tomatoes, and capers, and cook, stirring frequently with a wooden spoon, for about 4 minutes. Remove from the heat, cover, and set aside to rest.

In a small bowl, mix the cilantro with the remaining coconut oil to make a cilantro butter, mashing it with a fork to combine; set aside. Remove the stems from the mustard greens; they can be used as crudité or in another recipe.

In a large frying pan, bring about ½ cup water to a boil over high heat. Place the mustard leaves flat in the pan, one by one, and blanch for no longer than 2 seconds each.
Using tongs, transfer the leaves to the counter or a cutting board, spreading them flat.

When all the leaves have been blanched, stir about 2 to 3 tablespoons of the cilantro butter into the millet mixture to taste. (The leftover cilantro butter can be kept in the refrigerator for up to 1 week, or frozen in a tightly sealed container for up to 1 year.)

Divide the millet mixture evenly among the leaves, placing the filling at one end of each leaf; season with salt and pepper. Fold the sides over the filling and then roll like a burrito. Serve immediately.

EACH SERVING *343 calories (kcal) • 15 g fat • 0 mg cholesterol*
47 g carbohydrates • 8 g dietary fiber • 9 g protein • 321 mg sodium
2,629 IU vitamin A • 74 mg vitamin C • 85 mg calcium • 3 mg iron

ROASTED POTATOES AND CAULIFLOWER WITH ROMESCO SAUCE

Roasted potatoes are filling and make a balanced and spicy meal when paired with robust Spanish romesco sauce, made with almonds and red peppers, and green Romanesco cauliflower.

Makes 6 servings

INGREDIENTS

For the Romesco Sauce

2 large red bell peppers

¼ cup raw almonds, toasted

2 tablespoons extra-virgin olive oil

3 garlic cloves

1 teaspoon smoked paprika

¼ teaspoon cayenne pepper

Sea salt and freshly ground black pepper

For the Potatoes and Cauliflower

1 head Romanesco cauliflower (about 2 pounds), cored and chopped into 2-inch florets

1 pound small new potatoes, halved

2 tablespoons extra-virgin olive oil

1 teaspoon smoked paprika

Sea salt and freshly ground black pepper

Make the Romesco Sauce: Char the peppers over a gas flame or under a broiler until blackened and charred on all sides. Transfer to a bowl and cover with plastic wrap. Allow the peppers to steam for about 15 minutes or until cool enough to handle. Peel, seed, and stem the peppers. In a blender, puree the peppers along with the almonds, oil, garlic, smoked paprika, and cayenne until smooth. Season the sauce with salt and black pepper. (The romesco sauce can be prepared up to 1 week ahead. Transfer to a small plastic container and refrigerate.)

Make the Potatoes and Cauliflower: Preheat the oven to 400°F. In a large bowl, toss the cauliflower and potatoes with the oil to coat. Spread the vegetables out in a single layer on a large heavy baking sheet and sprinkle with the smoked paprika and salt and black pepper to taste. Roast until the cauliflower and potatoes are just beginning to brown, about 15 minutes. Stir the vegetables and continue to roast until golden brown and tender, about 10 minutes longer. Transfer the cauliflower and potatoes to a platter and serve with the romesco sauce.

EACH SERVING *170 calories (kcal) • 12 g fat • 0 mg cholesterol 15 g carbohydrates • 5 g dietary fiber • 3 g protein • 94 mg sodium 6,735 IU vitamin A • 63 mg vitamin C • 58 mg calcium • 1 mg iron*

CAULIFLOWER STEAKS WITH CREAMY PUREE AND GREMOLATA

The contrasting flavors and textures derived from the same vegetable in this caramelized cauliflower steak and creamy puree are surprising and satisfying. The gremolata, an herb-and-citrus garnish, adds a bright, fresh touch.

Makes 2 servings

INGREDIENTS

1 large cauliflower, leaves removed

6 ounces parsnips (about 2 medium), peeled and sliced

2 garlic cloves

1 bay leaf, preferably fresh

2 tablespoons extra-virgin olive oil

2 tablespoons finely chopped fresh flat-leaf parsley leaves

1 tablespoon capers, minced

1 tablespoon snipped chives

2 teaspoons fresh thyme leaves, finely chopped

½ teaspoon lemon zest

Sea salt and freshly ground black pepper

Place the cauliflower, stem-side up, on a cutting board. Using a large, sharp knife, cut the cauliflower through the stem into equal halves. Starting at the stem end of each half, thickly slice the cauliflower to create two ¾- to 1-inch-thick steaks. Break the remaining cauliflower into florets (you should have about 3 cups).

In a heavy medium saucepan, combine the cauliflower florets with the parsnips, 2 cups water, the garlic, and bay leaf over medium heat and simmer until the parsnips are very tender, about 20 minutes. Remove the bay leaf and transfer the parsnip mixture to a blender. Add 1 tablespoon of the oil and puree until smooth. Transfer back to the saucepan; set aside. (The puree and cauliflower steaks can be prepared up to 1 day ahead. Cover and refrigerate the puree and steaks separately.)

Meanwhile, make the gremolata: In a small bowl, gently stir together the parsley, capers, chives, thyme, and lemon zest to blend.

Preheat the oven to 400°F. Heat the remaining 1 tablespoon oil in a large cast-iron skillet over medium-high heat. Add the cauliflower steaks to the skillet and cook without moving them until they are browned on the bottom, about 4 minutes. Turn the steaks, sprinkle with salt and pepper, and cook for 4 minutes longer. Transfer the skillet to the oven and cook until the cauliflower steaks are tender and browned, about 20 minutes.

Meanwhile, bring the parsnip puree to a simmer over medium heat, stirring; season with salt and pepper. Divide the puree between two plates. Top with the steaks, sprinkle with the gremolata, and serve.

EACH SERVING *287 calories (kcal)* • *15 g fat* • *0 mg cholesterol*
35 g carbohydrates • *12 g dietary fiber* • *8 g protein* • *236 mg sodium*
431 IU vitamin A • *193 mg vitamin C* • *126 mg calcium* • *3 mg iron*

FORBIDDEN RICE WITH FAVA BEANS AND ASPARAGUS SPRING SAUTÉ

Whole-grain, antioxidant-rich, nutty-flavored forbidden rice topped with the crown jewels of the spring vegetable garden elevates this rice bowl to a higher plane.

Makes 4 to 6 servings

INGREDIENTS

For the Forbidden Rice

1 cup forbidden (black) rice

½ teaspoon sea salt

For the Spring Sauté

2 tablespoons plus 2 teaspoons extra-virgin olive oil

2 cups small shelled fresh or frozen fava beans (from about 1¾ pounds pods)

1 large shallot, minced

4 garlic cloves, minced

1 bunch asparagus (about 1 pound), cut on an angle into 1-inch pieces

1 tablespoon chopped fresh thyme

Sea salt and freshly ground black pepper

2 cups fava leaves, pea tendrils, or pea shoots

1 teaspoon balsamic vinegar

Make the Forbidden Rice: In a heavy medium saucepan, combine 1¾ cups water with the rice and salt and bring to a boil over high heat. Reduce the heat to low, cover, and simmer until the rice is tender and the water has been absorbed, about 30 minutes. Remove the rice from the heat and keep covered until ready to serve.

Meanwhile, prepare the Spring Sauté: Heat 2 tablespoons of the oil in a large heavy skillet over medium-high heat. Add the fava beans and stir-fry until lightly browned and blistered, about 4 minutes. Add the shallot and garlic and stir until fragrant, about 30 seconds. Stir in the asparagus, ⅓ cup water, and the thyme. Sprinkle with salt, cover, and cook until the water evaporates and the asparagus is crisp-tender, about 2 minutes. Season to taste with salt and pepper. Remove from the heat.

In a small bowl, toss the fava leaves with the remaining 2 teaspoons oil and the balsamic vinegar. Fluff the rice with a fork and spoon into serving bowls. Spoon the spring vegetable sauté over the rice, top with the fava leaves, and serve.

EACH SERVING (BASED ON 6 SERVINGS) *272 calories (kcal) • 7 g fat 0 mg cholesterol • 44 g carbohydrates • 6 g dietary fiber • 9 g protein • 168 mg sodium 1,183 IU vitamin A • 13 mg vitamin C • 59 mg calcium • 4 mg iron*

ZUCCHINI SPAGHETTI IN RICH GARLICKY SAUCE

This recipe is exciting because it's a pasta recipe without any pasta; it contains raw cacao powder, which adds richness and enough umami notes to keep your meat-eating friends satisfied; and it's heavy on the garlic, which contains a wealth of phytonutrients.

Makes 4 servings

INGREDIENTS

2 pounds zucchini (about 4 medium), tops and bottoms trimmed

2 tablespoons extra-virgin olive oil

2 small shallots, peeled and coarsely chopped

4 garlic cloves, crushed with a garlic press

3 cups coarsely chopped heirloom tomatoes (about 3 medium)

1 portobello mushroom, coarsely chopped

1 tablespoon dried oregano

1 teaspoon dried thyme

½ cup finely chopped fresh basil

2 tablespoons coconut sugar (see page 199) or honey

2 tablespoons raw cacao powder

1 teaspoon finely ground pink Himalayan salt

½ teaspoon coarsely ground black pepper

Finely grated Parmesan cheese or nutritional yeast, for serving (optional; see Note)

To transform the zucchini into pasta, shave off long fettuccine-like strips with the slicing blade of a box grater or shred into spaghetti using a spiralizer or mandoline (see Tip). Whatever method you use, let the pasta stand on parchment paper or on a clean kitchen towel to absorb excess moisture.

To prepare the sauce, gently heat the oil in a saucepan over low heat. Add the shallots and cook for 1 to 2 minutes, and then add the crushed garlic and cook for 1 to 2 minutes more. Stir in the tomatoes, mushroom, oregano, thyme, and basil, along with the sugar, cacao powder, salt, and pepper. Cover the pot and allow the sauce to simmer slowly, stirring occasionally with a wooden spoon, for at least 20 minutes and up to 2 hours to allow the flavors to meld.

Serve the sauce over the zucchini pasta. Sprinkle with grated Parmesan, if desired.

EACH SERVING *167 calories (kcal) • 9 g fat • 0 mg cholesterol*
21 g carbohydrates • 4 g dietary fiber • 4 g protein • 514 mg sodium
1,299 IU vitamin A • 54 mg vitamin C • 61 mg calcium • 2 mg iron

INGREDIENT NOTE *Nutritional yeast, also called yeast extract powder, is full of B vitamins, and its flavor and texture make it a satsifying vegan replacement for grated Parmesan cheese.*

COOK'S TIP *A spiralizer (also called a spiral slicer) is a kitchen tool specifically used to transform vegetables such as zucchini into long, fine strands, reminiscent of noodles.*

LENTIL AND WHOLE BEET STEW WITH ROSEMARY AND RED ONION

Beet root, stems, and leaves—the stems and leaves contain most of a beet's phytonutrients—are all cooked up in this hearty one-pot make-ahead meal.

Makes 4 to 6 servings

INGREDIENTS

8 small (2-inch-diameter) beets with green tops attached

2 tablespoons extra-virgin olive oil

1 red onion, chopped

6 garlic cloves, finely chopped

1½ cups green lentils, rinsed

2 cups low-sodium vegetable broth

1 teaspoon finely chopped fresh rosemary

½ teaspoon sea salt, plus more to taste

Freshly ground black pepper

Trim, peel, and cut the beets into quarters. Cut the stems into ½-inch pieces and tear the leaves into 3-inch pieces. (You should have about 6 cups leaves and stems.)

Heat the oil in a heavy medium Dutch oven over medium-high heat. Add the onion and garlic and sauté until the onion is golden brown, about 8 minutes. Stir in the lentils, 3 cups water, the broth, and the rosemary and bring to a boil. Reduce the heat to medium-low, cover, and simmer until the lentils are just beginning to soften, about 15 minutes. Add the beets and the salt. Return the stew to a simmer, cover, and cook until the lentils are soft but retain their shape and the beets are just tender, about 20 minutes. Stir in the beet leaves and stems, cover, and simmer until tender, about 7 minutes. Season the stew with salt and pepper, ladle into bowls, and serve. (The stew can be made up to 4 days ahead; cool, cover, and refrigerate. When you're ready to serve, reheat the stew over medium-low heat until simmering.)

EACH SERVING (BASED ON 6 SERVINGS) *243 calories (kcal) • 6 g fat 0 mg cholesterol • 38 g carbohydrates • 10 g dietary fiber • 12 g protein • 277 mg sodium 131 IU vitamin A • 6 mg vitamin C • 48 mg calcium • 4 mg iron*

MUSHROOM BOURGUIGNON

Spoon this hearty, comforting mushroom stew over whole wheat penne, quinoa, polenta, or roasted sweet potatoes.

Makes 4 servings

INGREDIENTS

2 tablespoons extra-virgin olive oil

1¼ pounds portobello or cremini mushrooms, cut into ¼-inch-thick slices

1 cup pearl onions, blanched in boiling water for 1 minute, drained, and peeled, or 1 cup frozen pearl onions, thawed

1 small carrot, unpeeled, chopped

½ yellow onion, chopped

1 tablespoon chopped fresh thyme

Sea salt and freshly ground black pepper

2 garlic cloves, minced

3 tablespoons balsamic vinegar

2½ cups low-sodium vegetable broth

1½ tablespoons tomato paste

1 bay leaf

1½ teaspoons cornstarch

2 tablespoons chopped fresh flat-leaf parsley leaves

Heat 1 tablespoon of the oil in a large heavy deep skillet over high heat. Add the mushrooms and pearl onions and sauté until the mushrooms begin to color, about 4 minutes. Transfer the vegetables to a bowl.

Add the remaining 1 tablespoon oil to the same skillet and place over medium heat. Add the carrot, yellow onion, and thyme. Sprinkle with salt and pepper. Cook until the onion is golden, about 8 minutes. Add the garlic and cook for 1 minute. Add the vinegar and scrape up any browned bits. Mix in the broth, tomato paste, and bay leaf. Return the mushrooms, pearl onions, and any accumulated liquid to the skillet. Reduce the heat, cover partially, and simmer until the mushrooms are very tender and the liquid has partially reduced, about 10 minutes.

Mix the cornstarch and 1 tablespoon water in a small cup. Add the slurry to the mushroom mixture and bring to a simmer. Cook until the sauce thickens, about 1 minute. Season to taste with salt and pepper. Sprinkle with the parsley and serve.

EACH SERVING, STEW ONLY *154 calories (kcal) • 8 g fat • 0 mg cholesterol 17 g carbohydrates • 3 g dietary fiber • 6 g protein • 114 mg sodium 2,372 IU vitamin A • 13 mg vitamin C • 41 mg calcium • 2 mg iron*

CHICKPEA BAJANE

"Bajane" is a Provençal term for the midday meal. Chickpeas are a staple in Provence; in this recipe, chickpeas, leeks, carrots, fennel, and spinach are served with nutty-tasting millet.

Makes 4 servings

INGREDIENTS

For the Bajane

1 tablespoon extra-virgin olive oil

1 large leek, white and green parts only, thinly sliced (about 2 cups)

4 garlic cloves, chopped

1 large fennel bulb, trimmed and diced

1 small bunch carrots, unpeeled, trimmed and sliced (about 1¾ cups)

½ teaspoon fennel seeds

1 (14½-ounce) can chickpeas, drained and rinsed

1 cup low-sodium vegetable broth

¼ cup fresh lemon juice

2 teaspoons chopped fresh thyme or summer savory

5 ounces baby spinach leaves

Sea salt and freshly ground black pepper

For the Millet

2 teaspoons extra-virgin olive oil

1 large garlic clove, minced

2½ cups low-sodium vegetable broth

1 cup millet

1½ teaspoons chopped fresh thyme or summer savory

¼ teaspoon sea salt

2 teaspoons fresh thyme leaves, for garnish

Make the Bajane: Heat the oil in a small heavy Dutch oven over medium-high heat. Add the leek and garlic and sauté until tender, about 8 minutes. Add the fennel, carrots, and fennel seeds, reduce the heat to medium, and sauté until the carrots and fennel are golden, about 10 minutes. Stir in the chickpeas, broth, lemon juice, and thyme. Cover and simmer over medium-low heat until the chickpeas are tender and the flavors develop, about 8 minutes. Top the bajane with the spinach, cover, and cook until the spinach just wilts, about 2 minutes. Season with salt and pepper.

Meanwhile, make the Millet: Heat the oil in large heavy saucepan over medium-high heat. Add the garlic and stir briefly. Add the broth, millet, chopped thyme, and salt. Cover and simmer over medium-low heat until the liquid has been absorbed and the millet is tender, about 20 minutes.

Divide the millet among shallow bowls; top with the bajane. Sprinkle with the fresh thyme leaves and serve.

EACH SERVING *432 calories (kcal) • 9 g fat • 0 mg cholesterol • 76 g carbohydrates 14 g dietary fiber • 13 g protein • 424 mg sodium • 11,480 IU vitamin A 30 mg vitamin C • 166 mg calcium • 6 mg iron*

SWEET POTATO–TURMERIC BLINI WITH POMEGRANATE AND SCALLIONS

The rich jewel-like colors of sweet potatoes are due to their high antioxidant content, and the darker the color of the flesh, the more phytonutrients they contain. The turmeric in this recipe brings even more pigment (and an anti-inflammatory boost) to the blini, so they're vibrant both aesthetically and from a health perspective.

Makes 2 servings

INGREDIENTS

2 large sweet potatoes (1¼ to 1½ pounds), peeled and chopped

2 teaspoons high-potency turmeric powder, or 2 tablespoons raw turmeric juice

½ teaspoon cayenne pepper

¼ cup dulse flakes

Sea salt and freshly ground black pepper

2 tablespoons unrefined virgin coconut oil

1 scallion, cut into ¾-inch pieces

½ to ¾ cup pomegranate seeds (from 1 medium pomegranate), whole or liquefied in a high-speed blender

Place the sweet potatoes in a pot and add enough water to cover. Bring to a boil over high heat. Cover the pot, reduce the heat to medium, and simmer until the potatoes are softened, about 15 minutes. Drain the potatoes and transfer to a medium bowl. Add the turmeric, cayenne, dulse, and salt and pepper to taste, then mash to create a smooth puree.

When the sweet potato mixture is cool enough to handle, form it into small balls and flatten these into discs that are about 2 inches wide and ½ inch thick. (You will have about 8 discs.)

In a cast-iron skillet, melt 1 tablespoon of the coconut oil over high heat, then fry the blini in batches, without crowding the pan, for about 8 minutes on the first side. Turn the blini over and fry for about 5 minutes more, until the blini are crisp and golden brown. Transfer to a paper towel–lined platter. Repeat until all the blini have been cooked.

In the same skillet, melt the remaining 1 tablespoon coconut oil over medium-high heat. Sauté the scallion until softened, 4 to 5 minutes.

Serve the blini topped with the scallions and the whole pomegranate seeds, pomegranate puree, or a combination.

EACH SERVING *453 calories (kcal)* • *16 g fat* • *0 mg cholesterol*
76 g carbohydrates • *14 g dietary fiber* • *8 g protein* • *108 mg sodium*
250 IU vitamin A • *61 mg vitamin C* • *112 mg calcium* • *3 mg iron*

GRILLED SWEET POTATOES WITH AVOCADO PIPIAN

Pipian, Spanish for "hulled pumpkin seed," is a traditional Mexican sauce that's similar to mole, and as with mole, there are countless variations. Here, the sauce relies on avocado for its creamy texture and full flavor. It's great on the sweet potato, but it also makes a delectable dip.

Makes 4 servings

INGREDIENTS

1¾ pounds dark-fleshed yams
(about 4 long, thin yams)

For the Pipian
1 poblano chile
1 small avocado, pitted, peeled, and diced
½ cup coarsely chopped fresh cilantro leaves
½ cup raw pepitas
1 scallion, trimmed and coarsely chopped

2 tablespoons fresh lime juice
1 garlic clove
½ teaspoon sea salt

Extra-virgin olive oil, for brushing
Ground cumin, for sprinkling
Sea salt and freshly ground black pepper
4 cups baby spinach or kale leaves
¼ cup raw pepitas, lightly toasted for garnish
½ cup fresh pomegranate seeds, for garnish

Bring a large pot of salted water to a rapid boil. Cook the yams until almost tender when pierced with a thin, sharp knife, about 15 minutes. Drain in a colander and let cool completely.

Meanwhile, make the Pipian: Char the poblano over a gas flame or under the broiler, turning it frequently until blackened and charred on all sides. Transfer to a small bowl, cover with a towel, and allow the chile to steam until cool enough to handle, about 30 minutes. Peel, seed, and stem the chile.

In the blender, combine the roasted poblano, avocado, cilantro, pepitas, scallion, lime juice, garlic, and salt. Add ½ cup water and puree. With the blender running, gradually add water by tablespoonfuls, up to ¼ cup more, to make a thick sauce. (The yams and sauce can be prepared up to 2 days ahead; cover separately and refrigerate.)

Preheat an outdoor grill to medium heat. Cut each yam into quarters lengthwise. Brush the yams with olive oil and sprinkle with the cumin and salt and pepper to taste. Grill the yams until browned and tender, turning occasionally, about 10 minutes.

Place 1 grilled yam on each plate and sprinkle with the baby spinach. Spoon the sauce over the yams. Sprinkle with the toasted pepitas and pomegranate seeds and serve.

EACH SERVING *475 calories (kcal)* • *25 g fat* • *0 mg cholesterol*
52 g carbohydrates • *12 g dietary fiber* • *17 g protein* • *342 mg sodium*
38,338 IU vitamin A • *155 mg vitamin C* • *217 mg calcium* • *6 mg iron*

EGGPLANT CANNELLONI WITH SPICY TOMATO-BASIL SAUCE AND CARAMELIZED ONIONS AND KALE

This is a good dish for entertaining as it can be made completely ahead. Try the mildly spicy tomato sauce on whole grain gluten-free pasta and sautéed kale if you are running short on time.

Makes 4 to 6 servings (12 rolls)

INGREDIENTS

For the Spicy Tomato-Basil Sauce

1 tablespoon extra-virgin olive oil

½ red onion, chopped

2 garlic cloves, chopped

¼ teaspoon crushed red pepper flakes

2 (15-ounce) cans diced tomatoes

2 tablespoons chopped basil leaves

Sea salt and freshly ground black pepper

For the Eggplant Rolls

2 large eggplants (about 18 ounces each), cut lengthwise into ¼-inch-thick slices

¼ cup plus 1 tablespoon extra-virgin olive oil

Sea salt

1 cup diced zucchini or yellow squash

1 cup diced red bell pepper

4 garlic cloves, minced

Freshly ground black pepper

2 cups cooked quinoa

¼ cup pine nuts

½ teaspoon dried oregano, crumbled

¼ cup low-sodium vegetable broth

For the Caramelized Onions and Kale

1 teaspoon extra-virgin olive oil

1 cup thinly sliced onions

¼ teaspoon crushed red pepper flakes

4 cups firmly packed torn kale leaves (about 4 ounces)

1 cup low-sodium vegetable broth

2 tablespoons minced garlic

1 teaspoon unfiltered apple cider vinegar

Sea salt and freshly ground black pepper

Make the Spicy Tomato-Basil Sauce: Heat the oil in a heavy medium saucepan over medium-high heat. Add the onion, garlic, and crushed red pepper and sauté for 2 minutes. Add the tomatoes and half of the basil and simmer until reduced to about 3 cups, stirring occasionally, about 20 minutes. Season to taste with salt and black pepper. Let cool, and then stir in the remaining basil. (The sauce can be made up to 1 day ahead; cover and refrigerate.)

Make the Eggplant Rolls: Preheat the broiler. Arrange the eggplant slices on two large baking sheets in a single layer. Using a pastry brush, lightly coat the eggplant slices with ¼ cup of the oil. Sprinkle with salt. Broil without turning until the eggplant is soft and slightly browned, watching carefully to prevent burning, about 5 minutes. Let cool completely.

Heat the remaining 1 tablespoon oil in a large heavy skillet over medium-high heat. Add the zucchini, bell pepper, and garlic and sauté until tender, about 5 minutes. Season to taste with salt and black pepper. Mix in the quinoa, pine nuts, and oregano. Stir in the broth, remove from the heat, and let cool. Using your hands, knead the quinoa stuffing mixture until all the ingredients are well moistened. Season to taste with more salt and black pepper.

On a work surface, place 1 eggplant slice, browned side facing down, with the wide, rounded end closest to you. Place 2 tablespoons of the stuffing on the rounded end and roll the eggplant up and away from you. Place the roll seam-side down on a large heavy baking sheet. Repeat with the remaining eggplant and stuffing. (The rolls can be made up to 1 day ahead; cover and refrigerate.)

Make the Caramelized Onions and Kale: Heat the oil in a large nonstick skillet over medium heat. Add the onions and crushed red pepper and cook until the onions are golden brown, stirring frequently, about 10 minutes. Add the kale, broth, and garlic and cook until the kale is tender and the mixture is caramelized, stirring occasionally, about 20 minutes. Add the vinegar and cook for 1 minute. Season to taste with salt and black pepper. (The kale and onions can be made up to 2 hours ahead. Set aside at room temperature.)

Preheat the oven to 350°F. Uncover the eggplant rolls, if refrigerated, and bake until heated through, about 15 minutes. Bring the tomato sauce to a simmer. Spoon about ⅓ cup of the sauce onto each serving plate and top each pool of sauce with 2 or 3 eggplant rolls. Spoon the caramelized onions and kale over the rolls and serve.

EACH SERVING (BASED ON 6 SERVINGS) *350 calories (kcal) • 20 g fat 0 mg cholesterol • 38 g carbohydrates • 9 g dietary fiber • 9 g protein • 443 mg sodium 5,098 IU vitamin A • 96 mg vitamin C • 146 mg calcium • 3 mg iron*

THE RANCH PUMPKIN PERSIMMON MEAT LOAF WITH MUSHROOM-SAGE PUMPKIN GRAVY

This is comfort food, pure and simple. It's made with traditional fall flavors, including pumpkin, mushroom, and sage, and is smothered in rich mushroom gravy.

Makes 1 large meat loaf (6 servings)

INGREDIENTS

1 cup green lentils

3 cups low-sodium vegetable broth or water

¾ teaspoon finely ground pink Himalayan salt, plus more to taste

1 cup walnuts, toasted

3 tablespoons raw pepitas

1 teaspoon grapeseed oil

3 garlic cloves, minced

1½ cups diced pumpkin

1 onion, diced

1 celery stalk, diced

1 carrot, scrubbed and grated

½ Fuyu persimmon (see Note) or green apple, grated

⅓ cup fresh or frozen cranberries, coarsely chopped

Preheat the oven to 350°F. Oil a large loaf pan and line with parchment paper.

Rinse the lentils and transfer to a small pot with the broth. Add the salt and bring to a rolling boil over high heat. Reduce the heat to medium-low and simmer, uncovered, stirring frequently and adding a little water if needed, until the lentils are slightly overcooked, 40 to 45 minutes. Pulse the lentils in a blender until mashed, but still chunky, or mash them by hand; set aside in large bowl.

Pulse the walnuts and pepitas in a blender until coarsely chopped, and add them to the bowl of lentils.

Heat the oil in a large skillet over medium heat. Sauté the garlic, pumpkin, and onion until the pumpkin is soft, about 5 minutes. Add the celery, carrot, persimmon, and cranberries. Sauté for about 5 minutes more, until the celery and carrots have softened.

Mix the sautéed vegetables and fruit into the nuts and lentils. Taste and add more salt if needed. Press the mixture firmly into the loaf pan, using a spatula to ensure that the corners are filled and the top is smooth.

Bake for 40 to 50 minutes, uncovered, until the edges are lightly browned. Cool in the pan for at least 10 minutes before transferring the meat loaf to a cooling rack. Slice and serve warm with gravy, or let cool completely.

MUSHROOM-SAGE PUMPKIN GRAVY

Makes 5 cups gravy

INGREDIENTS

1 tablespoon grapeseed oil

1 garlic clove, minced

1 tablespoon fresh chopped sage

2 cups fresh chanterelle or oyster mushrooms, cleaned and shredded in food processor

2 cups pure pumpkin puree (either homemade or canned)

2 cups low-sodium vegetable broth

3 bay leaves

Finely ground pink Himalayan salt and freshly ground black pepper

Put the oil in a medium saucepan over low heat and sauté the garlic, sage, and mushrooms for about 2 minutes. When the garlic is cooked, add the pumpkin puree to the pot. Add the broth and stir with a wooden spoon to combine. Add the bay leaves and season to taste with salt and pepper. Gently simmer for 10 to 15 minutes to allow the flavors to combine. Remove the bay leaves before serving. (This gravy can be made up to 5 days ahead; when cool, transfer to an airtight container and refrigerate. When ready to use, reheat over medium heat.)

EACH SERVING MEAT LOAF WITH GRAVY *438 calories (kcal) • 20 g fat 0 mg cholesterol • 52 g carbohydrates • 11 g dietary fiber • 18 g protein • 309 mg sodium 9,146 IU vitamin A • 13 mg vitamin C • 74 mg calcium • 5 mg iron*

EACH SERVING MEAT LOAF WITHOUT GRAVY *389 calories (kcal) • 17 g fat 0 mg cholesterol • 46 g carbohydrates • 10 g dietary fiber • 17 g protein • 260 mg sodium 4,437 IU vitamin A • 8 mg vitamin C • 51 mg calcium • 4 mg iron*

INGREDIENT NOTE *Fuyu persimmons are ripe when they are still firm, so they're perfect to cook with. They can be eaten whole, with their skins.*

MUSHROOM AND LEEK FRITTATA WITH PARSLEY AND CHIVES

This umami-packed frittata is great for dinner served with a green salad and the Ranch Balsamic Vinaigrette (page 111). Leftovers make a tasty cold lunch. Sautéing the mushrooms in batches allows for all the mushrooms to be cooked in the same skillet that the frittata gets cooked in.

Makes 6 servings

INGREDIENTS

3 tablespoons extra-virgin olive oil

3 leeks, white and pale green parts only, halved and sliced

12 ounces cremini mushrooms, sliced

12 ounces shiitake mushrooms, stemmed and sliced

8 ounces oyster mushrooms, sliced

3 large garlic cloves, minced

1 tablespoon tamari or soy sauce

6 to 8 large eggs, beaten to blend

¼ cup chopped fresh flat-leaf parsley

¼ cup snipped fresh chives

Freshly ground black pepper

Heat 1 tablespoon of the oil in a well-seasoned 9-inch cast-iron skillet over medium-high heat. Add the leeks and sauté until tender and golden brown, about 12 minutes. Transfer the leeks to a large bowl.

Add another tablespoon of the oil to the skillet (do not wash) and heat over medium heat. Add the cremini mushrooms and sauté until tender and reduced in volume, about 5 minutes. Add the shiitakes and sauté until tender and reduced in volume, about 5 minutes. Mix in the oyster mushrooms and continue to sauté until the mushrooms are tender. Stir in the garlic and sauté until the mushrooms and garlic are fragrant and tender, about 5 minutes. Stir in ¼ cup water and the tamari and stir until the liquid has been absorbed, about 3 minutes. Transfer the mushrooms to the bowl with the leeks.

Preheat the oven to 450°F. Heat the remaining 1 tablespoon oil in the same skillet (do not wash) over medium-high heat. Stir the eggs, parsley, and chives into the mushroom-leek mixture. Sprinkle with pepper and pour the mixture into the hot skillet; turn off the heat and let stand for 5 minutes. Transfer the skillet to the oven and cook until the eggs are cooked through and the frittata is firm to the touch, about 5 minutes longer. Let cool in the pan, cut into wedges, and serve warm.

EACH SERVING *204 calories (kcal) • 13 g fat • 187 mg cholesterol 12 g carbohydrates • 2 g dietary fiber • 12 g protein • 236 mg sodium 1,300 IU vitamin A • 13 mg vitamin C • 64 mg calcium • 3 mg iron*

TOMATO, BASIL, AND OLIVE PIZZA WITH CAULIFLOWER CRUST

The crust of this "pizza" is completely grain-free. In winter, sautéed onions and thyme leaves are a tasty replacement for the tomatoes and basil.

Makes two 7-inch pizzas

INGREDIENTS

Extra-virgin olive oil, for greasing

½ head cauliflower, separated into florets

1 cup grated vegan mozzarella or Jack cheese

1 large egg

2 tablespoons almond flour

2 garlic cloves, minced

¼ teaspoon crushed red pepper flakes

¼ teaspoon sea salt

2 tomatoes, sliced

⅓ cup pitted Kalamata olives, halved

6 large basil leaves, cut into fine ribbons

Preheat the oven to 450°F. Line a large heavy baking sheet with parchment paper. Coat lightly with olive oil.

Bring a medium saucepan of water to a boil. Place the cauliflower florets in a food processor with the metal blade attached. Pulse until the cauliflower is chopped into rice-size pieces. Cook 2½ cups of the cauliflower in the boiling water until tender, about 2 minutes. (Reserve the remainder for another use.) Drain in a fine-mesh strainer, then spread out on a large clean kitchen towel. When cool enough to handle, gather the towel together and squeeze as much water from the cauliflower as possible.

Transfer the cauliflower to a medium bowl. Add ½ cup of the cheese, the egg, almond flour, garlic, crushed red pepper, and salt and mix well. Divide the pizza dough in half and place in 2 mounds on the prepared baking sheet. Press and flatten each mound into a 7-inch round.

Bake the pizzas until crispy and golden, about 15 minutes. Sprinkle ¼ cup of the cheese over each pizza, then top with the tomatoes and olives. Bake until the cheese melts, about 6 minutes. Using scissors, cut the parchment in half to separate the pizzas. Slide each pizza on its parchment onto a plate. Using a metal spatula, slide the pizzas off the parchment. Sprinkle with basil and serve.

EACH 1-PIECE SERVING *137 calories (kcal)* • *7 g fat* • *47 mg cholesterol* • *16 g carbohydrates* • *3 g dietary fiber* • *5 g protein* • *453 mg sodium* • *698 IU vitamin A* • *54 mg vitamin C* • *71 mg calcium* • *1 mg iron*

MEDITERRANEAN VEGETABLE QUICHE WITH BUCKWHEAT CRUST

Buckwheat flour adds crumbliness and a delicious earthy flavor to any pastry. To ensure that pastry made with buckwheat flour binds properly, it's best to combine it in equal proportions with a less crumbly flour. For this crust, we pair it with spelt flour; a gluten-free all-purpose flour mix, such as Bob's Red Mill brand, would work, too.

Makes 8 servings

INGREDIENTS

For the Pastry

½ cup buckwheat flour

½ cup spelt flour

½ cup unrefined virgin coconut oil, at room temperature, plus extra for greasing

For the Filling

1 tablespoon olive oil

1 cup sliced mushrooms

1 cup cherry tomatoes, halved

½ cup thinly sliced leeks (white and pale green parts only)

1 medium zucchini, trimmed and thinly sliced

3 garlic cloves, crushed with a garlic press

1 teaspoon dried oregano

1 cup loosely packed fresh basil leaves, torn

1 cup canned tomato puree

Making the Pastry: In a large bowl, combine the buckwheat and spelt flours. Using a pastry blender or two butter knives, cut in the coconut oil (it should be solid but softened, a similar texture to room temperature butter). Continue to combine with your fingertips, lightly rubbing the oil into the flours to make a coarse crumb.

Transfer the crumb mixture to a greased 9-inch tart pan and press the mixture firmly onto the bottom and up the sides of the pan. For best results, refrigerate for 3 to 4 hours. Preheat the oven to 325°F, and then bake the crust for 10 minutes. Leave the oven on.

Meanwhile, make the Filling: Heat the oil in a large skillet over medium heat. Add the mushrooms, tomatoes, leeks, and zucchini, and sauté, stirring often with a wooden spoon, for about 8 minutes. Stir in the garlic, oregano, and basil and sauté for about 4 minutes more.

Transfer the vegetable mixture to the pastry shell and pour the tomato puree evenly over the vegetables. Bake for 10 to 12 minutes, until the edges of the crust are golden. Serve immediately.

EACH SERVING *207 calories (kcal) • 16 g fat • 0 mg cholesterol 15 g carbohydrates • 3 g dietary fiber • 4 g protein • 130 mg sodium 689 IU vitamin A • 14 mg vitamin C • 27 mg calcium • 2 mg iron*

RED PEPPER AND OLIVE SOCCA WITH CREAMY ZUCCHINI SAUCE

Socca is a crepe or flatbread made with chickpea flour that's popular in Provence and in Italy, where it is know as farinata. At the Ranch, the humble gluten-free pancake is embellished with peppers, olives, and fresh herbs and served with a creamy zucchini sauce.

Makes 4 servings

INGREDIENTS

¾ cup garbanzo bean flour

1 teaspoon sea salt

2½ tablespoons extra-virgin olive oil

12 ounces zucchini (about 2 small), trimmed and quartered lengthwise

2 garlic cloves, minced

¼ cup fresh flat-leaf parsley leaves

¼ cup almond milk, homemade (page 44) or unsweetened store-bought

1 red bell pepper, stemmed, seeded, and coarsely chopped

8 oil-cured black olives, pitted and halved

Scant 1 tablespoon fresh rosemary leaves

In a medium bowl, combine the flour and ½ teaspoon of the salt. Whisk in 1 cup water and 1 tablespoon of the oil. Cover the batter loosely with a clean kitchen towel and let stand at room temperature for 4 to 8 hours.

Preheat the oven to 450°F. In a well-seasoned 9-inch cast-iron skillet, toss the zucchini and half the garlic with 1 tablespoon of the oil. Roast the zucchini in the oven until browned and tender, about 10 minutes. (Do not turn off the oven.) Using tongs, transfer the zucchini and garlic to a blender. (Do not wash the skillet.) Add the parsley, almond milk, and remaining ½ teaspoon salt to the zucchini and puree until smooth; set the sauce aside.

In the same skillet, toss the bell pepper with the remaining garlic and remaining ½ tablespoon oil. Roast the pepper in the oven until tender and browned, about 10 minutes. Working quickly, distribute the peppers evenly over the bottom of the skillet with a wooden spoon. Pour the batter over the peppers. Sprinkle the surface evenly with the olives and rosemary and bake until golden brown and set, about 15 minutes. Cut the socca into wedges and serve immediately with the zucchini sauce.

EACH SERVING *179 calories (kcal) • 5 g fat • 0 mg cholesterol*
26 g carbohydrates • 7 g dietary fiber • 8 g protein • 54 mg sodium
11 IU vitamin A • 4 mg vitamin C • 68 mg calcium • 2 mg iron

AMARANTH CAKES WITH ASPARAGUS, ARTICHOKES, AND FENNEL

This recipe is a delightful taste of spring showcasing asparagus—the smaller the spears, the more nutritious they are, with the purple-tinged ones being the most nutritious of all— artichokes, and fennel. Baked, not fried, the dense amaranth cakes are a treat served with a fresh spring mesclun salad and plain yogurt. Amaranth is a seed, not a grain, which makes it naturally gluten-free and much higher in protein than most grains.

Makes 4 servings

INGREDIENTS

2½ cups low-sodium vegetable broth

1 cup amaranth

1 tablespoon hemp oil

2 thin asparagus spears, finely chopped

1 medium artichoke heart, finely chopped

¼ cup finely chopped fennel fronds

Sea salt and freshly ground black pepper

Preheat the oven to 400°F. Cut a sheet of parchment paper to fit a rimmed baking sheet and set aside. Alternatively, oil the baking sheet.

In a medium pan, bring the broth to a boil over high heat. Add the amaranth and oil. Cover, lower the heat, and slowly simmer for 20 to 25 minutes to make a sticky porridge. Remove the amaranth from the heat, and let it rest with the lid on for about 5 minutes.

Meanwhile, lightly wilt the asparagus, artichoke, and fennel by cooking them in a covered pan over low heat with about 2 tablespoons water, or enough to produce steam. Cook, stirring occasionally, until the vegetables are softened, 5 to 7 minutes. Add the amaranth to the pan and mix with a wooden spoon to combine it with the vegetables.

When the amaranth mixture is cool enough to handle, divide it into four equal parts and form into patties with your hands, placing each flattened patty on the prepared baking sheet.

Bake the amaranth cakes for about 20 minutes, then turn them over and bake for 10 to 15 minutes more, until golden brown. Serve hot.

EACH SERVING (I PATTY) *228 calories (kcal) • 7 g fat • 0 mg cholesterol 35 g carbohydrates • 4 g dietary fiber • 7 g protein • 114 mg sodium 112 IU vitamin A • 43 mg vitamin C • 95 mg calcium • 4 mg iron*

WALNUT CARNE WITH JICAMA SALAD AND CHIPOTLE GUACAMOLE

We've created a vegan meal that's rich in classic Mexican flavors and low on calories. Lime, cilantro, chile peppers, coriander, and cumin bring the sensuality of Latin cuisine to your kitchen, paired with lighter, plant-based ingredients such as jicama—a wonderful Mexican vegetable that tastes delicately sweet, is low in carbs, and is delicious eaten raw.

Makes 4 servings

INGREDIENTS

For the Walnut Carne

1 cup walnut pieces
(use black walnut if available)

1 portobello mushroom, coarsely minced

Juice of 2 limes

¼ cup loosely packed cilantro leaves and tender stems, finely minced

½ teaspoon ground coriander

¼ teaspoon ground cumin

1 teaspoon dried Mexican oregano
(Italian oregano can be substituted)

1 tablespoon olive oil

1 clove garlic

1 tablespoon honey

1 serrano chile, stemmed and finely minced

½ small red onion, finely minced

¼ teaspoon coarsely ground black pepper

1 teaspoon finely ground
Himalayan pink salt

For the Jicama Salad

½ medium jicama, unpeeled

½ medium fennel bulb, plus the fronds

12 asparagus spears

12 fresh cranberries

Juice of 1 medium orange

For the Chipotle Guacamole

2 ripe avocados, halved and pitted

1 very ripe tomato, diced

Juice of 1 lime

Leaves and tender stems from
½ bunch cilantro

½ medium red onion, minced

1 teaspoon chipotle chile powder
(see note, page 170)

Finely ground pink Himalayan
salt and freshly ground black pepper

Black Beans de Olla (optional, page 173)

Make the Walnut Carne: In a large nonreactive bowl, combine the walnut pieces and minced mushroom. Add the lime juice to the walnuts and mushrooms, along with the cilantro, coriander, cumin, oregano, oil, garlic, honey, chile, and onion. Stir to combine and season with the black pepper and salt. Set aside to marinate while you make the salad and salsa (see Tip).

Make the Jicama Salad: Leave the skin on the jicama and retain as much of the outer layers of the fennel bulb as possible. Thinly slice the jicama and fennel using a sharp knife or the slicing side of a box grater. Place the sliced jicama and fennel in a large nonreactive bowl. Chop the fennel fronds and add them to the bowl.

Chop the asparagus spears into 2-inch pieces as far down the spears as possible, discarding only the tough portions. Coarsely chop the cranberries, roughly into quarters. Add the asparagus and cranberries to the bowl with the jicama and fennel. Add the orange juice and toss to combine; set aside.

Just before serving, make the Chipotle Guacamole: Scrape the avocado flesh into a small nonreactive bowl and add the tomato, lime juice, cilantro, onion, and chipotle powder. Mash with a fork to combine and season with salt and black pepper to taste. Serve immediately.

Serve each component in separate bowls, allowing each person to mix flavors as they wish.

EACH SERVING WALNUT CARNE *264 calories (kcal) • 22 g fat • 0 mg cholesterol 14 g carbohydrates • 4 g dietary fiber • 8 g protein • 484 mg sodium 153 IU vitamin A • 16 mg vitamin C • 32 mg calcium • 1 mg iron*

EACH SERVING JICAMA SALAD *58 calories (kcal) • 0 g fat • 0 mg cholesterol 14 g carbohydrates • 5 g dietary fiber • 2 g protein • 17 mg sodium • 435 IU vitamin A 39 mg vitamin C • 47 mg calcium • 1 mg iron*

EACH SERVING GUACAMOLE *146 calories (kcal) • 12 g fat • 0 mg cholesterol 11 g carbohydrates • 6 g dietary fiber • 2 g protein • 18 mg sodium 507 IU vitamin A • 21 mg vitamin C • 19 mg calcium • 1 mg iron*

INGREDIENT NOTE *Chipotles are smoked chile peppers (usually jalapeños). Chipotle chile powder is a natural way to enjoy the flavor, and it's terrific in guacamole.*

COOK'S TIP *Consider making the Walnut Carne several hours ahead—a minimum of 2 hours and a maximum of 8 hours—to get the greatest health benefit from the nuts.*

SQUASH TACOS WITH POBLANO RAJAS AND BLACK BEANS DE OLLA

Rajas is a topping made from green chiles and cream. This vegan version is the perfect finish for this substantial Mexican favorite.

Makes 8 tacos

INGREDIENTS

For the Rajas

1 tablespoon extra-virgin olive oil

3 poblano chiles, stemmed, seeded, and sliced

1 onion, sliced

6 garlic cloves, chopped

1½ cups almond milk, homemade (see page 44) or unsweetened store-bought

1 teaspoon dried oregano

Sea salt

For the Squash Filling

1 (2½-pound) butternut squash, peeled, seeded, and cut into ½ by 2-inch pieces

2 tablespoons extra-virgin olive oil

1 tablespoon ancho chile powder

1 tablespoon ground cumin

Sea salt

About 2 cups Black Beans de Olla (recipe opposite) or canned vegetarian refried black beans

8 (6-inch) corn tortillas

Chopped fresh cilantro, for garnish

Prepared picante sauce, such as Valentina or Tio Pepe brands, for serving

Make the Rajas: Heat the oil in a large heavy saucepan over medium-high heat. Add the chiles and onion and sauté until golden brown and just tender, about 10 minutes. Add the garlic and sauté until tender, about 5 minutes. Reduce the heat to medium, stir in ½ cup water, and simmer until the water evaporates and the vegetables are very tender, about 3 minutes. Stir in the almond milk and oregano and simmer until the topping thickens and becomes creamy, about 5 minutes. Season to taste with salt. (The rajas can be made up to 4 days ahead; cover and refrigerate. To serve, stir over medium heat until heated through.)

Make the Squash Filling: Preheat the oven to 400°F. On a large heavy baking sheet, toss the squash with the oil, chile powder, and cumin. Sprinkle with salt and roast until the squash is just beginning to brown, about 15 minutes. Stir the squash and cook until browned and tender, about 15 minutes longer.

Heat the tortillas over an open gas flame or on a griddle. Top the tortillas with the black beans, about ¼ cup for each, and then the squash and rajas, dividing them evenly. Sprinkle the tacos with cilantro and serve with picante sauce.

BLACK BEANS DE OLLA

Olla refers to the pot that the beans are cooked in. Slow simmering and no presoaking results in dark black beans. Flavored simply with onions, garlic, bay leaves, and ancho chile powder, these beans are the perfect anchor in tacos, a great warming lunch, or a hearty black bean soup—just thin them with a little vegetable broth and puree.

Makes 6 cups (about 6 servings)

INGREDIENTS

2 tablespoons extra-virgin olive oil

1 large onion, chopped

4 garlic cloves, chopped

1 pound dried black beans, rinsed

3 bay leaves (preferably fresh)

2 teaspoons ancho chile powder

1 teaspoon sea salt

Heat the oil in a heavy medium Dutch oven or pot over medium heat. Add the onion and garlic and sauté until tender, about 8 minutes. Stir in the beans, and then add 8 cups water, the bay leaves, and the chile powder. Bring the beans to a simmer. Skim any foam from the top of the beans. Partially cover the pot and simmer the beans until very tender, stirring frequently, about 1½ hours. Stir in the salt and cook, uncovered, until creamy, about 20 minutes. (The beans can be prepared up to 3 days ahead and refrigerated, or frozen for up to 1 month.)

EACH 1-CUP SERVING *293 calories (kcal) • 6 g fat • 0 mg cholesterol*
46 g carbohydrates • 17 g dietary fiber • 16 g protein • 338 mg sodium
280 IU vitamin A • 3 mg vitamin C • 62 mg calcium • 4 mg iron

EACH TACO *256 calories (kcal) • 8 g fat • 0 mg cholesterol*
41 g carbohydrates • 9 g dietary fiber • 7 g protein • 139 mg sodium
13,248 IU vitamin A • 33 mg vitamin C • 135 mg calcium • 3 mg iron

MEZE PLATTER

It's a rare person who doesn't enjoy a Mediterranean meze platter: fresh hummus, baba ghanoush, juicy olives, tabbouleh, preserved lemons, tapenade, and more, all served with a glass of hot mint tea. It's a romantic feast with a unique intimacy because it's typically shared tapas-style from the same bowls.

GRAIN-FREE TABBOULEH SALAD

With our guests in mind, we've reimagined tabbouleh, creating a beautiful, nutrient-rich dish that retains all the flavor and satisfaction of the classic, without all those carbs and calories. The bulgur wheat has been replaced with raw grated cauliflower for a delicate, elegant tabbouleh that's lightly sweet in flavor. Try it—this salad is delicious, and never fails to win over the hearts and minds of even the most hardline tabbouleh fans.

Makes 4 servings

INGREDIENTS

1 garlic clove

3 Persian cucumbers, stems removed, diced

1 pint cherry tomatoes, quartered

Leaves and tender stems from 1 bunch flat-leaf parsley, coarsely chopped

½ cup fresh mint leaves and tender stems, finely chopped

3 scallions, minced

1 cup Kalamata olives, pitted and chopped

Juice of 1 lemon, plus more as needed

⅓ cup extra-virgin olive oil

½ teaspoon coarsely ground black pepper, plus more as needed

1 medium head cauliflower

Crush the garlic clove into a large bowl with a garlic press. Add the cucumbers, tomatoes, parsley, mint, scallions, and olives along with the lemon juice, oil, and pepper. Toss well to combine.

Using the coarse side of a box grater, grate the cauliflower florets onto a cutting board (you should have about 3½ cups grated cauliflower). Wrap the leaves and stems and refrigerate for another use.

Mix the grated cauliflower into the salad. Taste and adjust the lemon juice and black pepper before serving.

EACH SERVING *286 calories (kcal) • 23 g fat • 0 mg cholesterol*
20 g carbohydrates • 5 g dietary fiber • 4 g protein • 287 mg sodium
1,701 IU vitamin A • 77 mg vitamin C • 113 mg calcium • 3 mg iron

HEMPSEED BABA GHANOUSH

Serve this delicious dip with cucumber, celery, carrot sticks, and radish slices.

Makes 6 servings

INGREDIENTS

1 whole head garlic

2 tablespoons hemp oil

½ teaspoon ground cumin

1 large eggplant, or 2 small eggplants (about 1 pound)

3 tablespoons hempseed hearts (see Note, page 205)

Zest and juice of 1 lemon, plus more as needed

Sea salt

Honey to taste

Preheat the oven to 400°F.

Remove the outer layer of white papery skin from the garlic head, but do not separate the cloves or remove the papery skin that covers each clove. Place the whole garlic head on a 6-inch square piece of foil and drizzle with about 1 tablespoon of the hemp oil and sprinkle with the cumin. Wrap the foil around the garlic to seal.

Pierce the skin of the eggplant several times, and set it on a rimmed baking sheet along with the foil-wrapped garlic. Bake the eggplant and garlic for about 20 minutes. The eggplant is done when it has shrunk, the skin has shriveled, and the flesh is tender; the garlic cloves will have softened.

With a sharp knife, remove the stem and hard top of the eggplant and discard, then put the whole eggplant in a high-speed blender; do not blend yet. Open the foil and remove the garlic. Using a sharp knife, cut off the hard root ball from the base, then add the whole garlic to the blender. Add the remaining 1 tablespoon oil, the hemp hearts, lemon zest and juice, and salt to taste. Pulse to make a creamy paste, adding water 1 teaspoon at a time, if necessary, to create the desired dip consistency.

Taste the baba ghanoush and, if the dip needs to be sweetened, add honey, 1 teaspoon at a time, blending on high after each addition. More sea salt and lemon juice can be added to taste, too, if you like. (The baba ghanoush can be prepared up to 5 days ahead; store in an airtight container and refrigerate.)

EACH SERVING *118 calories (kcal) • 7 g fat • 0 mg cholesterol*
12 g carbohydrates • 5 g dietary fiber • 4 g protein • 4 mg sodium
43 IU vitamin A • 7 mg vitamin C • 23 mg calcium • 1 mg iron

SUPER BLACK HUMMUS

We love traditional hummus but decided to use black beans as the basis for this variation because of the high quantities of anthocyanins (powerful antioxidants) they contain. Black sesame seeds also contain anthocyanins and they're rich in calcium for healthy bones. We've also included plenty of parsley, another superfood due to its intense levels of green phytonutrients and detoxifying properties.

Makes 8 servings

INGREDIENTS

1 cup dried black beans

½ small yellow onion, unpeeled

1 teaspoon baking soda

2 garlic cloves, crushed with a garlic press

¼ cup chopped fresh flat-leaf parsley

⅓ cup raw black tahini (made from black sesame seeds; sesame tahini can be substituted)

Juice of ½ lemon

½ teaspoon sea salt

½ teaspoon ground cumin

½ teaspoon paprika

Extra-virgin olive oil, for serving

Soak the beans in water for at least 6 hours, or overnight. Drain and rinse.

In a large pot, combine the beans with about 1 cup water (it should completely cover the beans by about an inch), the onion, and baking soda. Cover, bring to a boil over high heat, and then lower the heat to maintain a simmer and cook the beans for about 45 minutes, regularly skimming the foam from the surface as they cook and replacing the lid each time.

When the beans are soft, with a slotted spoon, transfer the beans and onion to a food processor or high-speed blender. Do not discard the cooking water, which is rich with phytonutrients, and reserve 4 or 5 of the beans for the garnish.

Process the beans with some of the cooking water, adding the liquid 1 tablespoon at a time, until the beans are the desired consistency. Add the garlic, parsley, tahini, and lemon juice along with the salt, cumin, and paprika and process again to combine.

Transfer the hummus to a serving bowl, add a swirl of olive oil, and garnish with the reserved beans.

EACH SERVING *140 calories (kcal) • 6 g fat • 0 mg cholesterol 17 g carbohydrates • 6 g dietary fiber • 7 g protein • 338 mg sodium 240 IU vitamin A • 4 mg vitamin C • 36 mg calcium • 2 mg iron*

THE RANCH FALAFEL WITH TOMATO SALAD AND CASHEW TZATZIKI

Makes 4 servings

INGREDIENTS

For the Falafel

2 (13-ounce) cans chickpeas,
drained and rinsed

1 cup chopped onion

¼ cup chopped fresh cilantro leaves

¼ cup chopped fresh flat-leaf parsley leaves

3 tablespoons fresh lemon juice

3 garlic cloves

2 teaspoons ground cumin

2 teaspoons ground coriander

½ teaspoon cayenne pepper

½ teaspoon sea salt

¼ cup quinoa flakes

For the Tomato Salad

3 ripe tomatoes, diced

½ cup chopped red onion

¼ cup chopped fresh basil leaves

2 tablespoons red wine vinegar

1 tablespoon extra-virgin olive oil

Sea salt and freshly ground black pepper

Extra-virgin olive oil, for brushing

4 savoy, green, or red cabbage leaves

Cashew Tzatziki (page 181)

Make the Falafel: In a food processor with the metal blade attached, process the chickpeas with the onion, cilantro, parsley, lemon juice, garlic, cumin, coriander, cayenne, and salt until smooth. Transfer the chickpea mixture to a bowl and stir in the quinoa flakes. Form the mixture into twelve 2½-inch patties, about 3 tablespoons per patty. (The unbaked falafel patties can be made 1 day ahead; cover with plastic wrap and refrigerate.)

Make the Tomato Salad: In a medium nonreactive bowl, toss the tomatoes, onion, and basil with the vinegar and oil to coat. Season to taste with salt and pepper. Set aside.

Preheat the oven to 450°F. Brush a large heavy baking sheet with oil. Arrange the falafels on the prepared baking sheet and brush the tops very lightly with oil. Bake until the falafels are golden brown on the bottom, about 10 minutes. Carefully turn the falafels over with a slotted spatula and continue to bake until golden brown on both sides, about 5 minutes longer.

Place one cabbage leaf on each plate. Spoon the tzatziki into the cabbage leaves, about ¼ cup per cabbage leaf. Top the tzatziki with 3 falafels each. Garnish with the tomato salad and serve.

EACH SERVING *367 calories (kcal)* • *14 g fat* • *0 mg cholesterol*
50 g carbohydrates • *10 g dietary fiber* • *14 g protein* • *425 mg sodium*
1,398 IU vitamin A • *48 mg vitamin C* • *138 mg calcium* • *4 mg iron*

CASHEW TZATZIKI

Cashews replace yogurt in this vegan version of the traditional Greek sauce. Our cashew tzatziki is luscious on the Ranch Falafel (page 178), but it can also be enjoyed on grilled vegetables or as a dip for crudité.

Makes about 2 cups

INGREDIENTS

1 cup raw cashews

About 4 tablespoons fresh lemon juice

1 garlic clove

½ teaspoon sea salt

1 cup grated English (hothouse) cucumber (about ½ cucumber)

2 tablespoons chopped fresh dill

Soak the cashews overnight with enough water to cover by 2 inches.

Drain the cashews and transfer to a blender. Add ½ cup fresh water, 2 tablespoons lemon juice, the garlic, and the salt and puree until smooth. Transfer the cashew mixture to a bowl; stir in the cucumber and dill. Season to taste with the remaining lemon juice. (The tzatziki can be prepared up to 2 days ahead. Cover and refrigerate; stir before serving.)

EACH ¼-CUP SERVING: *103 calories (kcal) • 8 g fat • 0 mg cholesterol 7 g carbohydrates • 1 g dietary fiber • 3 g protein • 123 mg sodium 25 IU vitamin A • 4 mg vitamin C • 11 mg calcium • 1 mg iron*

VARIATIONS *Try adding ¼ cup finely chopped fresh flat-leaf parsley, or ¼ cup finely chopped shallots for an Arabic-style spin on this classic dish.*

ARTICHOKES WITH PRESERVED LEMONS

Artichoke hearts are too delicious not to enjoy in spring. They're also incredibly detoxing for the body, arriving every year just when we most need them, after the long winter months may have encouraged a little overindulgence. Preserved lemons are delicious; if you don't have the opportunity to preserve your own, they are available at specialty food stores. This is seasonal spring eating at its best, and is one of the easiest and most impressive dishes you can make!

Makes 4 servings

INGREDIENTS

16 baby artichokes
Juice of 2 lemons
1 preserved lemon (see recipe opposite or use store-bought)
¼ cup extra-virgin olive oil

Cut off the dark green stems, outer leaves, and pointed tips of the artichokes, then place the trimmed artichokes in a bowl. Pour the lemon juice over the artichokes and set aside to marinate for about 20 minutes.

Meanwhile, remove the peel of the preserved lemon and discard the flesh. Finely chop the peel and place in a bowl. Pour the olive oil over the lemon peel and mix to combine well.

Place the marinated artichokes in a large steamer inside a pot, and add water to reach just under the base of the steamer. Bring to a boil over high heat. Reduce the heat to low and steam, covered, for 15 to 20 minutes.

Remove from the heat, plate 4 artichokes on each plate, and drizzle with the preserved lemon sauce.

EACH SERVING *206 calories (kcal) • 14 g fat • 0 mg cholesterol*
19 g carbohydrates • 9 g dietary fiber • 5 g protein • 442 mg sodium
22 IU vitamin A • 28 mg vitamin C • 74 mg calcium • 2 mg iron

PRESERVED LEMONS

Preserved lemons are a Middle Eastern staple, ubiquitous from Casablanca to Istanbul. The whole fruit is preserved and, surprisingly, it's the lemon skins that are eaten, while the flesh is discarded. The skins develop a rich flavor that's an incredible addition to many recipes.

It's essential to use organic lemons: they haven't been waxed with any chemical pesticides, so their skins are safe to eat. The lemon juice combines with the salt to make a brine, fermenting the lemons to create a powerful food that, like sauerkraut or kombucha, is filled with live enzymes.

Makes one (½-gallon) jar (about 12 preserved lemons)

INGREDIENTS

20 to 24 lemons, depending on size and juiciness
1 pound coarse sea salt

Boil ½ gallon of water and pour it into a ½-gallon glass preserving jar. Let it sit for a few minutes to sterilize the jar, and then pour the water out. Wash the lid.

Pour a 1-inch layer of salt into the bottom of the jar. Cut 10 to 12 lemons in half and set aside. Cut a deep cross into each of the remaining 10 to 12 lemons, cutting from the pointed end of the fruit almost down to the stem, but not all the way through—you want the fruits to remain intact.

Add the lemons cut with crosses to the jar, one at a time, squashing each one down hard into the jar to occupy the space as optimally as possible and release its juices. After each lemon is added, top it with a generous layer of salt, about 1 inch, and then squeeze juice from the reserved lemon halves onto the pressed and salted lemons. Continue this process until the jar is filled, ending with a thick layer of salt on top.

Tightly seal the jar with the lid, and then turn the jar upside down to ensure that all the lemons are covered with the brine. Set the jar aside, right side up, in a cool, dark place for 1 week, opening the lid twice a day to allow the preserves to breathe. After a week, place the sealed jar in the refrigerator, and leave the lemons to mature for at least 6 weeks or up to 6 months before eating them.

OLIVE SUPERFOOD TAPENADE

Olives are celebrated for their abundant nutritional qualities, which have been linked to lower rates of heart disease. Although they are high in calories in relation to their weight, olives pack such a strong flavor punch that a little goes a long way. Supergreen micro food powders contribute protein and the micronutrients needed to rebuild cells. This tapenade is a tasty way to help your body.

Makes about 2 cups

INGREDIENTS

1½ cups olives, preferably raw-cured (see Note), pitted and finely chopped

2 large garlic cloves, peeled and crushed with a garlic press

1 teaspoon crushed red pepper flakes

2 tablespoons green powder, such as chlorella, barley grass, wheat grass, or spirulina

Pomegranate or red wine vinegar

In a bowl, mix the olives, garlic, crushed red pepper, and green powder to combine. Stir in vinegar, drop by drop, to create the desired consistency. Tapenade is a spread, not a sauce, so it's not necessary to add much liquid to thin it.

Serve with crudité vegetables and flax crackers for dipping.

EACH 1-TABLESPOON SERVING *13 calories (kcal) • 1 g fat • 0 mg cholesterol 1 g carbohydrates • 0 g dietary fiber • trace protein • 46 mg sodium 189 IU vitamin A • trace vitamin C • 0 mg calcium • 0 mg iron*

INGREDIENT NOTE *Raw-cured olives are our go-to at The Ranch due to their natural flavors, beautiful colors, and minimal processing. It's now possible to find raw-cured Moroccan black olives, huge purple Peruvian Botija olives, and juicy green olives. If you have the time and patience, it's worth pitting olives yourself for a richer flavor, but if not, this recipe will work perfectly with already pitted olives.*

VARIATIONS *Feel free to experiment with other vinegars, for example, balsamic or cider vinegar. Try any other kind of dried chile pepper that's available, adjusting the quantity to create the desired heat level. Or add ½ cup finely chopped sun-dried tomatoes.*

good and sweet

MOROCCAN-SPICED KALE CHIPS

Kale chips are easy to make and loved by all. They're great packed up for a road trip or enjoyed as a snack while you watch your favorite show, and the exotic spices also make them appropriate for an elegant appetizer. Ras el hanout is a Moroccan spice blend available at most supermarkets. If your store doesn't carry it, substitute ½ teaspoon each ground cumin and ground coriander and a pinch of cinnamon.

Makes about 24 chips

INGREDIENTS

1 tablespoon extra-virgin olive oil

½ teaspoon lemon zest

24 medium Tuscan kale leaves

Scant 1 teaspoon sea salt

1 teaspoon ras el hanout spice blend

1 teaspoon paprika

Preheat the oven to 250°F. In a large bowl, whisk the oil and lemon zest to blend. Add the kale and toss until the leaves are well coated on both sides. Arrange the kale in a single layer on two large heavy baking sheets.

Mix the salt, ras el hanout, and paprika in a small bowl. Sprinkle the spice mixture evenly over the kale. Bake until the kale leaves are crisp, about 30 minutes; cool on the baking sheets.

EACH SERVING (2 CHIPS) *20 calories (kcal) • 1 g fat • 0 mg cholesterol 2 g carbohydrates • 1 g dietary fiber • 1 g protein • 151 mg sodium 1,768 IU vitamin A • 20 mg vitamin C • 27 mg calcium • trace iron*

ANCHO-MAPLE SPICED NUT MIX

Smoky spiced nuts and seeds are good sprinkled on salad or on their own
as a nutrient-rich snack (see photo page 189).

Makes about 2 cups

INGREDIENTS

¼ cup raw almonds

¼ cup raw cashews

¼ cup raw pecans

¼ cup raw pepitas

¼ cup sunflower seeds

1 tablespoon maple syrup

1 teaspoon ancho chile powder

1 teaspoon ground cumin

½ teaspoon sea salt

Preheat the oven to 325°F. Line a large heavy rimmed baking sheet with a nonstick silicone
liner or parchment paper.

In a medium bowl, mix the almonds, cashews, pecans, pepitas, and sunflower seeds with the
maple syrup, chile powder, and cumin until well combined.

Spread the nut mixture evenly on the prepared baking sheet. Roast until lightly browned,
stirring once or twice, about 24 minutes. Transfer the pan to a wire rack and cool
completely. (The nut mix can be prepared up to 1 week ahead. Store in an airtight jar at
room temperature.)

EACH ¼-CUP SERVING *135 calories (kcal) • 11 g fat • 0 mg cholesterol
6 g carbohydrates • 2 g dietary fiber • 4 g protein • 175 mg sodium
103 IU vitamin A • 0 mg vitamin C • 21 mg calcium • 1 mg iron*

WATERMELON, LIME, AND HIBISCUS ICE POPS

Dried hibiscus flowers produce a lovely crimson-colored tea that makes an amazing refresher poured over ice on a summer day. It's super tart (and packed with vitamin C). Here we mellowed it with watermelon and turned it into ice pops that are fun for kids and adults.

Makes about 6 ice pops

INGREDIENTS

¼ cup dried hibiscus flowers (see Note)

2½ cups watermelon chunks (from about 1¼ pounds watermelon or ½ mini watermelon)

¼ cup raw agave nectar

½ teaspoon lime zest

3 tablespoons fresh lime juice

In a small saucepan, bring ¾ cup water and the dried hibiscus flowers to a simmer. Turn off the heat and let stand until cool. Pour through a fine-mesh sieve into a bowl.

In a food processor, blend the watermelon chunks until liquified. Strain through a fine-mesh sieve lined with muslin into a pitcher; discard any solids. (You should have about 1½ cups watermelon juice.)

Stir the hibiscus water, agave nectar, and lime zest and juice into the watermelon juice. Pour the juice mixture into ice pop molds and freeze until firm, about 7 hours.

EACH ICE POP *64 calories (kcal) • 0 g fat • 0 mg cholesterol • 16 g carbohydrates 0 g dietary fiber • 0 g protein • 1 mg sodium • 308 IU vitamin A 11 mg vitamin C • 4 mg calcium • 2 mg iron*

INGREDIENT NOTE *You can buy dried hibiscus flowers (also known as sorrel) in Indian, Latin, Caribbean, and Middle Eastern markets.*

COCONUT ICE CREAM
WITH PASSION FRUIT

This smooth ice cream is a cool indulgence for special occasions. Passion fruit grows on pretty vines at The Ranch. The pulp boasts significant amounts of beta-carotene, vitamin C, and fiber, and a tart, floral flavor that's a winning contrast to the sweet coconut. If you can't get your hands on a passion fruit, the ice cream is good layered with banana, kiwi, and mango slices to create a tropical banana split, or simply top with fresh berries.

Makes about 1 pint

INGREDIENTS

1 (13.5-ounce) can organic coconut milk

6 tablespoons raw agave nectar

3 tablespoons unsweetened shredded coconut

2 teaspoons fresh lime juice

About ¾ cup passion fruit pulp (from about 6 passion fruits), for serving

In a medium bowl, whisk together the coconut milk, agave nectar, shredded coconut, and lime juice to blend. Process the coconut milk mixture in an ice cream maker according to the manufacturer's directions. (The ice cream can be frozen in an airtight container for up to 1 month.)

Let the ice cream soften slightly at room temperature before serving in bowls with the passion fruit pulp.

EACH ⅓-CUP SERVING *232 calories (kcal) • 17 g fat • 0 mg cholesterol 22 g carbohydrates • 3 g dietary fiber • 2 g protein • 13 mg sodium 12 mg calcium • 1 mg iron • 115 IU vitamin A • 5 mg vitamin C*

AÇAÍ AND POMEGRANATE GRANITA

Eat dessert and grow younger? Antioxidant-rich açaí berries from South America blend with vitamin-packed pomegranate in this sophisticated frozen dessert that may have anti-aging properties. Garnish the granita according to your fancy. At The Ranch, kumquat trees grow in abundance so we like to add a zesty pop of color and tart flavor; pomegranate seeds are pretty and tasty, too. For a really decadent (but still good for you!) treat, try drizzling the dessert with a little coconut milk.

Makes 4 servings

INGREDIENTS

1 (3.5-ounce) package frozen açaí puree, such as Sambazon or Amafruits, thawed

1 cup pomegranate juice

2 tablespoons raw agave nectar

About 8 tablespoons canned unsweetened coconut milk (optional)

Pomegranate seeds, for garnish (optional)

Sliced kumquats, for garnish (optional)

In a medium bowl, stir the açaí puree, pomegranate juice, and agave nectar to blend. Pour the açaí mixture into an 8½ by 4½-inch loaf pan. Freeze until slushy, about 1 hour; stir with a fork. Return the granita to the freezer and freeze until firm, stirring once or twice along the way, about 40 minutes more. (The granita can be made up to 1 week ahead; cover tightly with one layer of plastic wrap and store in the freezer.)

When you're ready to serve, use a fork or a grapefruit spoon to scrape the surface of the granita, creating icy flakes. Spoon into bowls; do not pack. If desired, drizzle the granita with the coconut milk, and garnish with the pomegranate seeds and kumquat slices.

EACH SERVING (WITHOUT COCONUT MILK) *84 calories (kcal) • 0 g fat 0 mg cholesterol • 21 g carbohydrates • 0 g dietary fiber • 0 g protein 9 mg sodium • 62 IU vitamin A • 3 mg vitamin C • 13 mg calcium • 0 mg iron*

EACH SERVING (WITH COCONUT MILK) *139 calories (kcal) • 7 g fat 0 mg cholesterol • 21 g carbohydrates • 0 g dietary fiber • 1 g protein 12 mg sodium • 62 IU vitamin A • 3 mg vitamin C • 18 mg calcium • 1 mg iron*

CRYSTALLIZED GINGER AND TURMERIC

When eaten in moderation, this is a wonderful treat that can satisfy any cravings for candy. When handling turmeric, avoid cutting it on plastic or wooden chopping boards—it's a strong dye.

Makes about 2 cups

INGREDIENTS

2 ounces fresh ginger, unpeeled,
cut into ½-inch pieces (about 1 cup)

2 ounces fresh turmeric, unpeeled, cut into
½-inch pieces (about 1 cup)

2 cups coconut sugar (see Note)

⅔ cup honey

Put the ginger and turmeric in a medium pot with just enough water to cover. Bring to a boil over high heat, and cook, uncovered, adding more water occasionally to keep them covered, until softened, about 1 hour.

Stir in 1 cup of the coconut sugar, lower the heat, and simmer for 10 minutes more. Remove from the heat and let stand at room temperature to cool completely.

Add the remaining 1 cup coconut sugar and enough water to cover, and return to a simmer over medium heat. Simmer for 10 minutes, and then let stand to cool again.

Meanwhile, place a 16-ounce mason jar in a pot along with the lid, add water to cover, bring to a boil, and boil for 10 minutes to sterilize the jar and lid. Using tongs, remove the jar from the water and let stand to drip-dry.

Add the honey to the pot with the ginger and turmeric, stir well to combine, and add enough water to cover the ginger and turmeric. Return to a simmer over medium heat and simmer until the liquid forms a thick syrup to coat the ginger and turmeric pieces, about 10 minutes. Stir occasionally to make sure the syrup doesn't burn.

Using a metal spoon, transfer the ginger and turmeric, along with any remaining syrup, to the sterilized mason jar, screw on the lid, and let stand to cool completely. (The crystallized ginger and turmeric will keep at room temperature, tightly sealed in the mason jar, for several months.)

EACH 2-TABLESPOON SERVING *70 calories (kcal) • 0 g fat • 0 mg cholesterol 18 g carbohydrates • 0 g dietary fiber • 0 g protein • 22 mg sodium 0 IU vitamin A • 4 mg vitamin C • 2 mg calcium • 0 mg iron*

VARIATION *Try coating the crystallized ginger and turmeric pieces with a melted raw chocolate made from equal amounts cacao butter, coconut sugar, and cacao powder. Dip the pieces in the chocolate mixture, arrange on a baking sheet, and freeze for about 5 minutes before serving.*

INGREDIENT NOTE *Coconut sugar is a traditional heirloom ingredient from Indonesia. It is rich in minerals, with a relatively low glycemic index compared with refined sugar or raw agave syrup.*

CHAI-POACHED PEARS

All four of the chai spices—cinnamon, ginger, cardamom, and black pepper—promote good health and improve digestion; in addition, they bring a sense of warmth and comfort. Fragrant, exotic, and exquisitely delicious, they are the perfect match for these classic poached pears, which can be enjoyed as a light breakfast, afternoon snack, and, of course, dessert.

Makes 4 servings

INGREDIENTS

2 cinnamon sticks

1 (2-inch) piece fresh ginger, crushed with a knife to crack the skin

20 cardamom pods, cracked

24 black peppercorns

4 firm but ripe medium-sized pears

In a pot large enough to hold the 4 pears, combine 10 cups water with the cinnamon sticks, ginger, cardamom, and peppercorns. Bring the water to a rolling boil, reduce the heat to maintain a simmer, cover, and continue simmering for 20 minutes to infuse the water with the spices.

Wash the pears and cut them in half, leaving the peels on and cores and stems intact. Add the pears to the spice-infused water, cover the pot, and simmer until they are poached. They should be tender enough that a knife easily pierces them but they still hold their shape; this can take from 45 minutes to 2 hours. The duration varies depending on the variety of the pears and the ripeness of the fruit. Let sit in the poaching liquid, with the lid on the pot, for about 30 minutes until the pears are cool enough to serve. As the pears steep, the chai-spiced liquid will continue to infuse the fruit.

To serve, plate two pear halves per person. Spoon some of the poaching liquid over the pears.

EACH SERVING *104 calories (kcal) • 0 g fat • 0 mg cholesterol 28 g carbohydrates • 6 g dietary fiber • 1 g protein • 2 mg sodium 51 IU vitamin A • 8 mg vitamin C • 19 mg calcium • trace iron*

COOK'S TIP *The chai-spiced poaching liquid becomes a warming beverage when strained and served in a teacup. It's also refreshing served over ice in a tall glass with a cinnamon stick.*

PEANUT BUTTER BUTTONS

Reminiscent of a peanut butter cookie but with a texture similar to shortbread, these rich and nutritious gluten-free vegan cookies make a good post-hike snack or late-morning energy boost. Almond butter can stand in for the peanut butter if peanut allergies are an issue.

Makes about 2 dozen cookies

INGREDIENTS

1 cup creamy peanut butter, such as Santa Cruz Organics

½ cup raw agave nectar

¼ cup unrefined virgin coconut oil, melted

¾ teaspoon sea salt

1¼ cups oat flour

½ cup flaxseed meal (see Note)

Preheat the oven to 350°F.

In a medium bowl, using a fork, stir together the peanut butter, agave nectar, coconut oil, and salt to blend. Mix in the oat flour and flaxseed meal until well combined.

Roll the dough into 1-inch balls. Transfer the balls to two ungreased large heavy baking sheets, making sure they are evenly spaced; flatten slightly to create 1½-inch rounds. Bake until golden brown, about 12 minutes. Transfer the cookies to a wire rack to cool. (The cookies can be prepared up to 3 days ahead; store in an airtight container at room temperature.)

EACH 1-COOKIE SERVING *134 calories (kcal) • 9 g fat • 0 mg cholesterol 11 g carbohydrates • 2 g dietary fiber • 4 g protein • 110 mg sodium 0 IU vitamin A • 0 mg vitamin C • 15 mg calcium • 1 mg iron*

INGREDIENT NOTE *Flaxseed meal, ground flaxseed, is available at most supermarkets now. The meal has a delightful nutty-sweet flavor, sometimes resembling banana. Flaxseed meal is very versatile. High in omega-3 fatty acids, lingans, and fiber, flaxseed meal is great for lower-fat baking. It can also be used as an egg substitute.*

BITTERSWEET CHOCOLATE BARK WITH PISTACHIOS, GOJI, AND GINGER

Part indulgence, part health food, this crunchy, earthy-yet-elegant treat is an instant mood-lifter on a hike, an impressive hostess gift, or a stylish finish to a fine meal. Cocoa nibs are bits of the roasted cocoa bean—they add crunch, magnesium, and intense chocolate flavor to the bark without adding sugar. They are also rich in antioxidants, iron, and magnesium. Feel free to play around with the toppings, making substitutions to suit your taste.

Makes about 12 pieces

INGREDIENTS

8 ounces bittersweet chocolate (72% cacao), chopped

4 tablespoons toasted salted hempseeds (see Note)

2 tablespoons dried blueberries

2 tablespoons dried goji berries (see Note, page 51) or dried cherries

2 tablespoons roasted shelled pistachios

2 tablespoons walnut pieces

2 tablespoons thinly sliced crystallized ginger (for homemade, see page 198)

1 tablespoon cocoa nibs

Fleur de sel, for sprinkling

Line a small baking sheet with aluminum foil. In a small heavy saucepan over very low heat, stir the chocolate until melted and smooth. Mix in 3 tablespoons of the hempseeds. Pour the chocolate onto the prepared baking sheet and, using a spatula, spread to form an approximately 7 by 10-inch rectangle.

Sprinkle the melted chocolate with the dried blueberries, goji berries, pistachios, walnuts, ginger, cocoa nibs, and remaining 1 tablespoon hempseeds. Scatter a few fleur de sel crystals on top of the chocolate.

Refrigerate the bark until the chocolate sets, about 30 minutes. Peel the foil off the back of the chocolate and coarsely chop the bark into 12 pieces. Transfer the bark to a jar and seal. (The bark can be refrigerated for up to 3 weeks.)

EACH PIECE *172 calories (kcal)* • *11 g fat* • *0 mg cholesterol*
15 g carbohydrates • *1 g dietary fiber* • *3 g protein* • *25 mg sodium*
91 IU vitamin A • *0 mg vitamin C* • *8 mg calcium* • *1 mg iron*

INGREDIENT NOTE *Hempseeds are sold hulled at natural foods stores. With a slightly sweet and nutty flavor, the seeds add protein and all of the essential amino acids to cereals, salads, and baked goods.*

CHOCOLATE MOUSSE

The cacao used to make this luscious chocolate mousse is just a nut inside a fruit, so if you don't mix it with sugary ingredients, and instead pair it with healthful ingredients, it's actually good for you!

Makes 8 servings

INGREDIENTS

½ cup hempseed hearts (see Note)

2 tablespoons raw agave nectar

½ teaspoons organic vanilla extract

¾ cup raw cacao powder

1 cup mesquite powder (see Note)

¾ cup unrefined virgin coconut oil, melted but not cooled

In a blender set to the highest speed, blend the hemp, ½ cup water, the agave nectar, and the vanilla extract until liquefied, about 2 minutes.

Using a fine-mesh sieve, strain the cacao and mesquite powders into a bowl, crumbling any clumps to produce a fine flour. Add the warm coconut oil to the powders and mix with a metal spoon to blend.

Using a spatula and working quickly, fold the blended hemp into the cacao-mesquite mixture to form a glossy, thick liquid mousse. Pour into eight bowls and serve immediately, while the mousse is still slightly warm from the coconut oil.

EACH SERVING *339 calories (kcal) • 28 g fat • 0 mg cholesterol*
16 g carbohydrates • 8 g dietary fiber • 4 g protein • 11 mg sodium
0 IU vitamin A • 0 mg vitamin C • 40 mg calcium • 2 mg iron

INGREDIENT NOTE: *Hempseed hearts are hempseeds that have been hulled. Hempseeds are considered a complete protein and the creamy-colored and -textured hearts, flecked with green and black, are the most nutritious part. They have a delicious flavor that's reminiscent of sesame.*

INGREDIENT NOTE *Long used as a sweetener by the Native Americans, before European settlers brought sugar, mesquite powder actually stabilizes the blood sugar by supporting the body's own production of insulin. Mesquite powder can be purchased at natural foods stores and online.*

MENU PLANNER
OUR RESULTS-BASED WEEKLY MENU PLANNER
FOR DETOXIFICATION AND WEIGHT LOSS

Weekly menu plans from The Ranch can be enjoyed at home—including irresistible flavors and all the health benefits of the recipes. You can also visit The Ranch to take part in the entire health and wellness program.

The Ranch's menu includes plant-based recipes averaging about 1,100 calories a day for women and 1,300 calories a day for men. The difference is in the portion size. Men receive portions 25 percent larger than women. The recipes can easily be part of maintaining a healthy lifestyle.

The Ranch has a garden where seasonal fruits and vegetables are grown year-round. The garden provides a variety of foods served as snacks, desserts, side dishes, and main courses. Beverages are offered all day and include herbal teas, and fruit- and vegetable-flavored waters.

WEEK ONE

Monday

BREAKFAST Ranch Granola with ½ cup Almond Milk *(409 calories)*

LUNCH Whole Onion and Carrot Soup *(41 calories)*,
Radicchio and Kohlrabi Salad with Avocado and Egg *(159 calories)*

DINNER Polenta with Roasted Acorn Squash Ragout *(344 calories)*

SNACK Moroccan-Spiced Kale Chips *(80 calories)*, seasonal fruit *(80 calories)*

ESTIMATED DAILY CALORIES *1,113–1,392 calories*

Tuesday

BREAKFAST Oats and Teff with Cardamom and Peaches *(182 calories)*

LUNCH Quinoa Salad with Spring Vegetables and Herbs *(288 calories)*

DINNER Eggplant Wraps with Muhamara and Tahini Sauce *(487 calories)*

SNACK Ancho-Maple Spiced Nut Mix *(135 calories)*, seasonal vegetable *(25 calories)*

ESTIMATED DAILY CALORIES *1,117–1,396 calories*

Wednesday

BREAKFAST Tibetan Tsampa *(363 calories)*

LUNCH Grilled Artichokes with Garlic Broth and White Bean Brandade *(252 calories)*

DINNER Forbidden Rice with Fava Beans and Asparagus Spring Sauté *(272 calories)*

SNACK Açaí and Pomegranate Granita *(84 calories)*, raw almonds *(132 calories)*

ESTIMATED DAILY CALORIES *1,103–1,379 calories*

Thursday

BREAKFAST Fresh Turmeric-and-Spice-Infused Almond Milk *(80 calories)*,
seasonal fruit *(80 calories)*

LUNCH Kale and Chickpea Salad with Pickled Red Onions *(464 calories)*

DINNER Mediterranean Vegetable Quiche with Buckwheat Crust *(207 calories)*

SNACK Coconut Ice Cream with Passion Fruit *(232 calories)*,
seasonal vegetable *(25 calories)*

ESTIMATED DAILY CALORIES *1,088–1,360 calories*

Friday

BREAKFAST Blistered Tomato and Spinach Scramble *(103 calories)*,
Wake-Up! Kale Juice *(147 calories)*

LUNCH Tofu, Cabbage, and Miso Soup *(186 calories)*,
Asian Slaw with Spicy Peanut Dressing *(130 calories)*

DINNER Squash Tacos with Creamy Poblano Rajas and
Black Beans de Olla *(256 calories)*

SNACK Peanut Butter Buttons *(134 calories)*, seasonal fruit *(80 calories)*

ESTIMATED DAILY CALORIES *1,036–1,295 calories*

Saturday

BREAKFAST Blueberry-Almond Oat Muffins *(212 calories)*

LUNCH Curried Cauliflower and Warm Spelt Salad *(200 calories)*

DINNER The Ranch Pumpkin Persimmon Meat Loaf with
Mushroom-Sage Pumpkin Gravy *(438 calories)*

SNACK Bittersweet Chocolate Bark with Pistachios, Goji, and Ginger *(172 calories)*,
seasonal vegetable *(25 calories)*

ESTIMATED DAILY CALORIES *1,047–1,309 calories*

Sunday

BREAKFAST Berry Breakfast Smoothie *(165 calories)*

LUNCH Korean Kelp Noodles with Napa Cabbage and Asian Pears *(318 calories)*

DINNER Mustard Green Wraps with Garlicky Millet and Tomatoes *(343 calories)*

SNACK Watermelon, Lime, and Hibiscus Ice Pop *(64 calories)*,
raw almonds *(132 calories)*

ESTIMATED DAILY CALORIES *1,022–1,278 calories*

WEEK TWO

Monday

BREAKFAST Avocado Toasts with Micro Greens and Sesame *(253 calories)*

LUNCH Whole Leek Soup *(181 calories)*,
Hijiki Salad with Pumpkin and Tamari Sauce *(125 calories)*

DINNER Indian-Spiced Swiss Chard Rolls with Coconut Tomato Sauce *(338 calories)*

SNACK Chai-Poached Pears *(104 calories)*, seasonal vegetable *(25 calories)*

ESTIMATED DAILY CALORIES *1,026–1,283 calories*

Tuesday

BREAKFAST Raw Oatmeal with Almonds and Fruit *(385 calories)*

LUNCH Hearts of Palm and Watercress with Balsamic Dressing *(222 calories)*

DINNER Collard Green Sushi with Curry-Tahini Dipping Sauce *(324 calories)*

SNACK Crystallized Ginger and Turmeric *(70 calories)*, raw almonds *(132 calories)*

ESTIMATED DAILY CALORIES *1,133–1,416 calories*

Wednesday

BREAKFAST Sweet and Chewy Multigrain Fruit and Nut Bar *(301 calories)*

LUNCH Mexican Fruit Salad with Chili Salt *(117 calories)*, seed crackers *(56 calories)*

DINNER Mushroom Bourguignon *(154 calories)* with whole wheat penne *(87 calories)*

SNACK Chocolate Mousse *(339 calories)*, seasonal fruit *(80 calories)*

ESTIMATED DAILY CALORIES *1,134–1,418 calories*

Thursday

BREAKFAST Buckwheat-Flax Pancakes with Walnuts and Maple Syrup *(96 calories)*

LUNCH Cauliflower Soup *(100 calories)*, Collard Greens,
Sprouts, and Goji Berry Salad *(147 calories)*

DINNER Sweet Potato–Turmeric Blini with Pomegranate and Scallions *(453 calories)*

SNACK Açaí and Pomegranate Granita *(84 calories)*, raw almonds *(132 calories)*

ESTIMATED DAILY CALORIES *1,012–1,265 calories*

Friday

BREAKFAST Sweet Potato Muffins with Coconut Crystals *(214 calories)*

LUNCH Super Black Hummus *(140 calories)* with
seed crackers *(112 calories)* and seasonal vegetable *(50 calories)*

DINNER Lentil and Whole Beet Stew with Rosemary and Red Onion *(243 calories)*

SNACK Ancho-Maple Spiced Nut Mix *(135 calories)*, seasonal fruit *(80 calories)*

ESTIMATED DAILY CALORIES *974–1,218 calories*

Saturday

BREAKFAST Gingered Pineapple, Celery, and Romaine Smoothie *(126 calories)*

LUNCH The Ranch Detox Salad with Purple Dressing *(112 calories)*

DINNER Walnut Carne with Jicama Salad and Chipotle Guacamole *(468 calories)*

SNACK Coconut Ice Cream with Passion Fruit *(232 calories)*, raw almonds *(132 calories)*

ESTIMATED DAILY CALORIES *1,070–1,338 calories*

Sunday

BREAKFAST Gluten- and Sugar-Free Banana Bread with 1 tablespoon peanut butter *(259 calories)*

LUNCH Creamy Vegan Tomato and Basil Soup *(281 calories)*,
Warm Brussels Sprout Caesar *(130 calories)*

DINNER Amaranth Cakes with Asparagus, Artichokes, and Fennel *(228 calories)*

SNACK Moroccan-Spiced Kale Chips *(80 calories)*, seasonal fruit *(80 calories)*

ESTIMATED DAILY CALORIES *1,058–1,323 calories*

WEEK THREE

Monday

BREAKFAST Spiced Cranberry Hazelnut Granola with ½ cup Almond Milk (*204 calories*)

LUNCH Whole Leek Soup (*181 calories*), Grain-free Tabbouleh Salad (*286 calories*)

DINNER Artichokes with Preserved Lemons (*206 calories*)

SNACK Peanut Butter Buttons (*134 calories*), raw almonds (*132 calories*)

ESTIMATED DAILY CALORIES *1,143–1,429 calories*

Tuesday

BREAKFAST Shine On! Juice (*179 calories*)

LUNCH Golden Sesame Sea Vegetable Soup (*268 calories*),
White Bean Salad with Olives and Arugula (*287 calories*)

DINNER Grilled Sweet Potatoes with Avocado Pipian (*475 calories*)

SNACK Watermelon, Lime, and Hibiscus Ice Pop (*64 calories*), seasonal vegetable (*25 calories*)

ESTIMATED DAILY CALORIES *1,298–1,623 calories*

Wednesday

BREAKFAST Oats and Teff with Cardamom and Peaches (*182 calories*)

LUNCH Thai Larb with Cauliflower and Coconut Rice in Lettuce Cup (*240 calories*)

DINNER Risotto with Mushrooms, Roasted Kabocha Squash, and Parsnips (*362 calories*)

SNACK Bittersweet Chocolate Bark with Pistachios,
Goji, and Ginger (*172 calories*), seasonal fruit (*80 calories*)

ESTIMATED DAILY CALORIES *1,036–1,295 calories*

Thursday

BREAKFAST Go Green! Juice *(202 calories)*

LUNCH Hempseed Baba Ghanoush *(118 calories)*
with seed crackers *(112 calories)* and seasonal vegetable *(50 calories)*

DINNER Eggplant Cannelloni with Spicy Tomato-Basil Sauce and
Caramelized Onions and Kale *(350 calories)*

SNACK Chai-Poached Pears *(104 calories)*, raw almonds *(132 calories)*

ESTIMATED DAILY CALORIES *1,068–1,333 calories*

Friday

BREAKFAST Buckwheat-Flax Pancakes with Walnuts and Maple Syrup *(96 calories)*

LUNCH The Ranch Falafel with Creamy Cashew Tzatziki and Tomato Salad *(367 calories)*

DINNER Chickpea Bajane *(432 calories)*

SNACK Crystallized Ginger and Turmeric *(70 calories)*, seasonal vegetable *(25 calories)*

ESTIMATED DAILY CALORIES *990–1,238 calories*

Saturday

BREAKFAST Berry Breakfast Smoothie *(165 calories)*

LUNCH Tomato, Basil, and Olive Pizza with Cauliflower Crust *(2 slices; 274 calories)*

DINNER Nettle and Basil Pesto with Walnuts and Whole-Grain Pasta *(442 calories)*

SNACK Ancho-Maple Spiced Nut Mix *(135 calories)*, seasonal fruit *(80 calories)*

ESTIMATED DAILY CALORIES *1,096–1,370 calories*

Sunday

BREAKFAST Avocado Toasts with Microgreens and Sesame *(253 calories)*

LUNCH Mushroom and Leek Frittata with Parsley and Chives *(204 calories)*

DINNER Cauliflower Steaks with Creamy Puree and Gremolata *(287 calories)*

SNACK Chocolate Mousse *(339 calories)*, seasonal vegetable *(25 calories)*

ESTIMATED DAILY CALORIES *1,108–1,385 calories*

CONVERSION CHART

All conversions are approximate.

Liquid Conversions

U.S.	METRIC	U.S.	METRIC
1 tsp	5 ml	1 cup	240 ml
1 tbs	15 ml	1 cup + 2tbs	275 ml
2 tbs	30 ml	1¼ cups	300 ml
3 tbs	45 ml	1⅓ cups	325 ml
¼ cup	60 ml	1½ cups	350 ml
⅓ cup	75 ml	1⅔ cups	375 ml
⅓ cup + 1 tbs	90 ml	1¾ cups	400 ml
⅓ cup + 2 tbs	100 ml	1¾ cups + 2 tbs	450 ml
½ cup	120 ml	2 cups (1 pint)	475 ml
⅔ cup	150 ml	2½ cups	600 ml
¾ cup	180 ml	3 cups	720 ml
¾ cup + 2 tbs	200 ml	4 cups	945 ml
		(1 quart)	(1,000 ml is 1 liter)

Weight Conversions

U.S./U.K.	METRIC
½ oz	14 g
1 oz	28 g
1½ oz	43 g
2 oz	57 g
2½ oz	71 g
3 oz	85 g
3½ oz	100 g
4 oz	113 g
5 oz	142 g
6 oz	170 g
7 oz	200 g
8 oz	227 g
9 oz	255 g
10 oz	284 g
11 oz	312 g
12 oz	340 g
13 oz	368 g
14 oz	400 g
15 oz	425 g
1 lb	454 g

Oven Temperatures

°F	GAS MARK	°C
250	½	120
275	1	140
300	2	150
325	3	165
350	4	180
375	5	190
400	6	200
425	7	220
450	8	230
475	9	240
500	10	260
550	Broil	290

INDEX

C

cabbage: green, 98; Napa, 118; recipe
        featuring, 82–83; red, 98, 178

cacao powder, raw, 18, 144, 205

candy, 198–99, 203

cannellini beans, 100, 122–23

capers, 96, 137, 140–41

cardamom, 47, 200; about, 30; recipe
        featuring, 49

carrots, 69, 98, 100, 106, 108–9, 121,
        128–33, 149, 150, 158–59; about, 21;
        purple, 21, 76–77; recipe featuring,
        76–77

cashew(s), 78, 90, 112, 181, 191; about, 32;
        chèvre, 89–90; milk, 32

cauliflower, 18, 19, 104–5, 106, 121, 130–31,
        175; about, 21; recipes featuring, 80,
        138, 140–41, 162

celery, 69, 158–59; recipe featuring, 67

celiac disease, 16, 34, 35, 105

cereals, 48–51

cherries, dried, 203; sour, 52–53, 93

chia seeds, 69

chickpeas, 178; about, 30, 32; recipes
        featuring, 108–9, 150

chile powder, 191; chipotle, 169–70

chives, 74, 112, 140–41; recipe featuring, 161

chlorella, 102, 184

chocolate, bittersweet, 203

chocolate mousse, 40, 205

cilantro, 80, 86, 98, 104–5, 121, 130–33,
        135–36, 137, 152–53, 169–70, 172–73,
        178; recipe featuring, 114

cinnamon, 40, 43, 48, 57, 59; about, 30;
        sticks, 47, 128–29, 200

cocoa nibs, 203

coconut: chips, 43; crystals, 57; grated,
        130–31; milk, 128–29, 130–31, 195,
        196; light, 121; oil, unrefined virgin,
        40, 43, 50–51, 52–53, 54, 57, 59,
        104–5, 132–33, 137, 151, 163, 202,
        205; recipes featuring, 128–29, 195;
        shredded, 195; sugar, 132–33, 144,
        198–99; unsweetened shredded, 40,
        52–53

collard greens, recipes featuring, 102,
        132–33

conversion chart, 214

cookies, 202

coriander, 121, 169–70, 178

cranberries: about, 29; dried, 43, 106, 126–
        27; fresh, 106, 158–59, 169–70; recipes
        featuring, 43

cucumbers, 70, 86; English, 130–31, 132–33,
        181; Persian, 175; pickled, 34

cumin, 104–5, 121, 128–29, 152–53, 169–70,
        172–73, 176, 177, 178, 191; seeds,
        crushed, 135–36

currants, dried, 88

curry powder, 80, 128–29; recipe featuring,
        132–33

D

dairy, whole, 16

dandelion leaves, 26

dates, 40, 112; Medjool, 54

desserts, 192–205

devil's claw, 32

dill, 79, 94–95, 112, 113, 181

dulse, 26, 79; flakes, 151

J

Jack cheese, vegan, 162
jalapeño, 121
jicama, 86; about, 22; recipe featuring, 169–70
juice variations, 69–70

K

kabocha, 99, 120
kaffir lime leaves, 121, 130–31
Kalamata olives, 100, 162, 175
kale, 64, 70, 106, 152–53; about, 22, 25; curly, 132–33; recipes featuring, 70, 108–9, 155–56, 188
kaniwa, about, 33
kelp noodles, 79, 118
kimchi, 34
kiwi, 70
kombu, 74
kosher salt, 55, 59
kumquats, 196

L

lecithin, vegan non-soy, 45
leeks, 74, 150, 161, 163
lemon(s), 56, 70, 94–95, 122–23, 182–83; recipe featuring, 113; recipe for preserved, 182–83; zest, 90, 94–95, 96, 113, 115, 122–23, 140–41, 176, 188
lemongrass, 121
lentils: green, 146, 158–59; recipe featuring, 146
lime(s), 69, 104–5, 169–70; recipe featuring, 192; zest, 118, 192

live cultures, 34, 36
loganberries, 29
lotus root, 99
lutein, 26

M

maca, 18, 30, 45, 115
magnesium, 33
manganese, 33
mangoes, 86
maple syrup, 19, 40, 43, 57, 59, 109, 191; recipe featuring, 60
marionberries, 29
Medjool dates, 54
menu planner, 207–13
mesquite, 19; powder, 205
Mexican recipes, 86, 169–73
meze platter, 175–84
micro greens, Asian, 56
Middle Eastern recipes, 135–36, 175–84
millet, 52–53, 137, 150; about, 33
minerals, trace, 79
mint leaves, 94–95, 135–36, 175, 196
mirin, 99
molasses, light, 52–53
Moroccan black olives, 184
mozzarella, vegan, 162
mushrooms, 163; about, 25; Asian, 99, 120; Bourguignon, 149; chanterelle, 159; cordyceps, 25; cremini, 120, 149, 161; enoki, 118; maitake, 120; oyster, 159; portobello, 144, 149, 169–70; powdered, 25; recipes featuring, 159, 161; shiitake, 120, 161
mustard: coarse-grain, 111; Dijon, 85, 96

N

Napa cabbage, 118

nasturtium flowers and leaves, 94–95

nasunin, 21

nettle leaves, 125

nori, 26, 79, 82–83

nutmeg, 40, 43

nuts: about, 32. *See also specific types*

O

oat flour, 202

oats, 40, 43, 48, 52–53, 59, 60; about, 33–34;
    recipe featuring, 49

olives: green, 108–9; Kalamata, 100, 162,
    175; oil-cured black, 164; raw-cured,
    184; recipes featuring, 100, 162

onions, 80, 99, 122–23, 126–27, 128–29,
    149, 155–56, 158–59, 172–73, 173,
    178; about, 25; pearl, 149; recipe
    featuring, 76–77; red, 76–77, 88, 100,
    108–9, 109, 146, 155–56, 169–70, 178;
    yellow, 78, 177. *See also* leeks; scallions

orange(s), 43, 69, 70, 102; about, 29; recipe
    featuring, 114; zest, 114, 132–33

oregano, 144, 155–56, 163, 172–73;
    Mexican, 169–70

organic foods, 15; fruits and berries, 29;
    vegetables, 19, 21

P

papain, 86

papayas: green, 98; Mexican, 86

paprika, 138, 177, 188

Parmesan cheese, grated, 144

parsley, 70, 76–77, 96; flat-leaf, 120, 122–23,
    140–41, 149, 164, 175, 177, 178; recipe
    featuring, 161

parsnips, 120, 140–41

passion fruit pulp, 195

pea tendrils or shoots, 142

peaches, 49

peanut butter, creamy, 98, 202

peanut oil, 130–31

peas, sugar snap or snow, 94–95

pecans, 40, 52–53, 191

pepita milk, 32

pepitas, 106, 152–53, 158–59, 191; about, 32

persimmon, Fuyu, 158–59

phenolics, 21

phytonutrients, 15, 18, 19, 21, 25, 26, 29,
    34–35, 82–83, 106, 146, 151

picante sauce, 172–73

pickled vegetables, 34–35

pine nuts, 88, 155–56

pineapples, 64, 69, 86; recipe featuring, 67

pistachios, 203

pizza, 162

plums, dried, 48

poblano chiles, 152–53, 172–73

pomegranate: molasses, 136; recipes
    featuring, 151, 196; seeds, 151, 152–
    53, 196; vinegar, 184

potassium, 36

potatoes, new, 138

probiotic capsules, 48

prunes. *See* plums, dried

pumpkin: puree, 159; recipes featuring, 99,
    158–59

Purple Dressing, 106, 115

Q

quercetin, 22, 25

quiche, 163

quinoa, 18, 155–56; about, 33; flakes, 136, 158–59, 178; recipe featuring, 94–95; red, 93

R

radicchio, recipes featuring, 85, 93

radish greens, 82–83

radish tops, 94–95

radishes, 94–95

raisins, 128–29; golden, 52–53

ras el hanout spice blend, 188

raspberries, 29, 64

raw foods, eating, 18

red shiso leaves, 82–83

red wine vinegar, 88, 93, 109, 178, 184

reishi, 25, 30, 45

rice: black (forbidden), 142; puffed brown, 52–53

rice vinegar, 113, 118

risotto, 120

Romaine lettuce, 26, 69; recipe featuring, 67

Romanesco cauliflower, 138

rosemary, 90, 122–23, 164; recipe featuring, 146

S

sage, 120, 126–27; recipe featuring, 159

salad dressings, 88, 96, 98, 108–9, 111–15

salads, 85–109

sauerkraut, 34

savory, 150

Savoy cabbage, 82–83

scallions, 63, 80, 82–83, 94–95, 98, 118, 128–29, 130–31, 152–153, 175; recipe featuring, 151

sea vegetables, 99; about, 26; recipe featuring, 79

seeds, 32. *See also specific types*

serrano chile, 169–70

sesame oil, 56, 82–83, 100, 108–9, 118

sesame seeds, 79, 82–83, 100, 108–9, 118; about, 32; recipe featuring, 56

shallots, 79, 93, 104–5, 120, 121, 122–23, 130–31, 137, 142, 144

sherry wine vinegar, 100, 108–9, 126–27

shoyu, 35–36, 118

Siberian kale, 25

smoothies, 64, 67

snacks, 52–53, 188, 191

socca, 164

sorbitol, 48

sorrel. *See* hibiscus flowers, dried

soups, 74–83

soy sauce, 35–36, 96, 98, 121

spaghetti, whole-grain, 125

spelt: flour, 163; recipe featuring, 104–5

spices: about, 30. *See also specific types*

spinach, 70, 106, 130–31, 135–36, 150, 152–53; about, 26; recipe featuring, 63

spirulina, 102, 184

squash: about, 26; acorn, 126–27; butternut, 99, 120, 172–73; recipe featuring, 172–73; yellow, 155–56

Sriracha sauce, 98

stevia, 19

strawberries, 60, 64

ACKNOWLEDGMENTS

We would like to thank the guests of The Ranch, who come with open hearts and minds to "unplug and reset"—while pushing themselves to new levels of health and wellness—and who for years have asked us to create a cookbook.

We are grateful for our very loyal and dedicated Ranch staff, who fill each day with joy, inspiration, and accomplishment. This book would not be possible without the chefs, past and present, who have taken healthy food to new heights, including Kurt Steeber, Rob Dalzell, Alexx Guevara, and Meredith Haaz.

Special thanks to Christopher Krubert, MD, for his support and passion in all that we do, and to Lisa Wolf for being authentically you.

And to our talented book team: Jill Cohen, who brought our dream to fruition and managed the process flawlessly through completion; Ysanne Spevack and Jeanne Kelley, who wrote, tested, and developed the recipes; Sara Remington, whose photography brilliantly captures the organic beauty of our food and garden; Dr. Sandra Frank, for her expert research and nutritional analysis; our Rizzoli editors, Christopher Steighner and Tricia Levi; and our contributors, assistants, and stylists, including Shelly Smedberg, Ethel Brennan, Nicole Rejwan, Sarah Tenaglia, Lydia Burkhalter, and Elizabeth Hyland. And a special thanks to our talented designers, Doug Turshen and Steve Turner.

We are endlessly grateful to Melissa Amerian, and Allyn and Susan Magrino, along with our entire dynamic Magrino team, and we appreciate all of the media that have been so integral to our success with their amazing support of The Ranch, including Kate Betts, Joyce Chang, Dany Levy, Nancy Novogrod, and Linda Wells.

And to everyone who helped make The Ranch possible from construction to opening, including Scott Shrader, Lisa Collins, Michael Lee, Steven Gambrel, Lisa Bowles, Ellen Francisco, JoAnn Kurtz-Ahlers, Susan Young, Solange Willems, and Denise Schipper.

Above all, we thank our parents, who gave us the confidence to follow our dreams.

First published in the United States of America in 2015
by Rizzoli International Publications, Inc.
300 Park Avenue South
New York, NY 10010
www.rizzoliusa.com

All photographs by Sara Remington
Cover illustration by Julia Rothman
Design by Doug Turshen with Steve Turner

2015 2016 2017 2018 / 10 9 8 7 6 5 4 3 2 1

Distributed in the U.S. trade by Random House, New York

Printed in China

ISBN-13: 978-0-8478-4485-2

Library of Congress Catalog Control Number: 2014952654